PRAISE FOR *THE BACKPACKER'S*

Learning journeys include sudden transitions between places – the sort of changes that can make your head spin with culture shock. *The Backpacker's Guide to University* presents a highly readable mix of tips and tricks that is deeply rooted in a wealth of experience and serious research under its calming, glossy surface.

Imagine going to a tropical beach for the first time. You can go with a professional diver who will be pointing out the most incredible creatures of the coral reef, while safely steering you around the hungry sharks and paralysing jellyfish. This book sets out a similarly safe course through academic waters: it explains things before you go, as you are on the journey, and offers help if you get in trouble. Avoiding things that bite or sting as you jump in is profoundly logical.

And let's face it, any good teacher or lecturer will tell you to read widely: to read about the subject content, read about processes, read for fun, and even read about reading. It makes total sense to take this guide with you to university – reading it will help you be more ready!

Dr Arjun Reesink, secondary school teacher and university academic

The Backpacker's Guide to University is a practical and accessible book for any student who is about to progress into higher education. It provides a clear and concise set of tips and advice on how to approach and navigate the different spheres of becoming a university student.

The book is particularly helpful for students who are unsure about what is expected of them – with useful and practical prompts, scenarios and highlights that illustrate and make explicit what one can do. The central message is for students to be open and to embrace new or different experiences, and the analogy of the backpacker promotes a transformative mindset.

Complete with tasks and activities, this guide is a comprehensive toolkit for navigating the varied slopes and terrains of student life – translating insight into actionable advice. It's an essential book to slip into your backpack on the way to university!

Billy Wong, Professor of Education, University of Reading, and author of *The Ideal Student*

The prospect of going to university can feel daunting – a step change in independence, autonomy and unfamiliar academic systems that may contrast sharply with school experiences. Nevertheless, for many, it becomes a rich and even transformative chapter in their life.

In *The Backpacker's Guide to University*, Jo and Martin offer practical, down-to-earth advice for new undergraduates. With a clear structure – covering pre-arrival preparation, first-term tips and 'emergency' guidance for when things feel overwhelming – the book is designed to help students not just survive but thrive. Like seasoned travellers, readers are encouraged to relish the journey, not just the destination.

Highly recommended reading for Year 13s and a thoughtful, confidence-boosting gift for friends and family members about to start university.

Ben White, secondary school leader, education consultant and co-author of *The Next Big Thing in Education*

The Backpacker's Guide to University is refreshingly honest about the huge difference between secondary school and university, while also introducing this new life stage as an entirely doable adventure. Phillips and Griffin serve as friendly, respectful mentors who demystify the language of higher education and suggest small but meaningful steps to help grow confidence – from weekly scheduling to handling demoralising feedback to building concentration. This book connects the practical and emotional aspects of learning to learn, and cheers on the reader to embrace the unique experience of university life. The most practical and positive guide you could wish for: 100% encouraging.

Professor Clare Rishbeth, University of Sheffield

A fantastic resource to help students shift their mindsets during the transition to university. The combination of essential information alongside practical activities will empower students and set them up for success.

Dr Jen McGahan, Senior Lecturer, Manchester Metropolitan University

The Backpacker's Guide to University is an immersive, helpful roadmap to all aspects of university written by professionals who know what it's like. The experiences and advice shared by the authors relate to the struggles and worries that many students may feel, packaged into an excellent guide for this new journey of life with its solutions and reflections. The inspiring messages and engaging tasks help to develop students' confidence and help them make the most out of their time in university by empowering them to become active participants in their learning.

This book makes the prospect of going to university something to be excited about, rather than terrified. It's perfect for new undergraduates and any university students who need a bit of guidance and encouragement.

Emily Barber, sixth-form student and writer

The Backpacker's Guide to University is an invaluable resource for first-year students and the university staff who support them. It is readable and fun, but most importantly it is filled with practical and relevant activities that cover the very real experiences that so many first-year students face. With this book, as a first-year you will set yourself on the fast track to self-awareness and personal growth and will receive those key insights and pointers that many students wish they had received when starting out.

Embracing the metaphor of the backpacker's journey, the authors invite students to view university as a life adventure and encourage students to begin their next chapter with courage, curiosity and hope.

A must-read for anyone embarking on the university adventure.

Fanie Walters, first-year lecturer and Head of Residence – Erica, University of Pretoria

With its straightforward and practical advice, *The Backpacker's Guide to University* is an essential resource for students embarking on their university journey.

One of the book's strongest aspects is its focus on mapping workspaces – an insightful section that highlights how environment plays a crucial role in productivity and wellbeing. The guidance on mixing, acculturating and acclimatising to a new setting is invaluable, equipping students with the tools to adjust both socially and academically. Equally impressive is the advice on how and where to get support, ensuring students feel confident in accessing help when needed. The discussions on interaction and navigating impostor syndrome further enrich the book, offering reassuring perspectives on belonging and self-confidence.

This is a much-needed book for students seeking both practical advice and emotional support during their university years. For anyone looking for a clear, actionable roadmap to settling in and thriving, *The Backpacker's Guide to University* comes highly recommended. A must-have companion for the journey ahead.

Karl Smith, Principal, Rochdale Sixth Form College

THE BACKPACKER'S GUIDE TO UNIVERSITY

AN UNDERGRADUATE'S GUIDE TO TRAVELLING WELL AND STAYING THE COURSE

DR JO PHILLIPS AND MARTIN GRIFFIN

Crown House Publishing Limited
www.crownhouse.co.uk

First published by
Crown House Publishing Limited
Crown Buildings, Bancyfelin, Carmarthen, Wales, SA33 5ND, UK
www.crownhouse.co.uk

and

Crown House Publishing Company LLC
PO Box 2223, Williston, VT 05495, USA
www.crownhousepublishing.com

EU GPSR Authorised Representative
Appointed EU Representative: Easy Access System Europe Oü, 16879218
Address: Mustamäe tee 50, 10621, Tallinn, Estonia
Contact Details: gpsr.requests@easproject.com, +358 40 500 3575

British Library Cataloguing-in-Publication Data

A catalogue entry for this book is available from the British Library.

Print ISBN 978-178583744-9
Mobi ISBN 978-178583770-8
ePub ISBN 978-178583771-5
ePDF ISBN 978-178583772-2

LCCN: 2025940834

Printed in the UK by
CMP, Poole, Dorset

Thank you to Diane, John, Liz and Peter for supporting
us through our education, and to Aggie, who we hope
will find joy and fulfilment in the journey.

ACKNOWLEDGEMENTS

Thanks to all the hardworking staff at Crown House Publishing who've contributed to improving this text. David Bowman gave us the go-ahead, Beverley Randell and Tom Fitton provided patient feedback and asked all the right questions, and Louise Penny spent many an hour with the pages, going through every word with focus and dedication. Thanks as well to Elen Martin and Lucy Delbridge for their work. Special thanks to Laura Jazwinski, our terrific illustrator, for all the time she spent discussing the project and for every beautiful image she's produced. And, of course, thanks go to every student we've ever taught, for everything they have, in turn, taught us.

CONTENTS

ABOUT US

Before we start, a little about us – your guides for this trip of a lifetime!

Dr Jo Phillips taught in five different sixth form colleges, then moved into higher education. She has been teaching in universities for the last fifteen years. This puts her in a rare position – she's taught A level students and hundreds of undergraduates too. Often, university lecturers don't have experience in school or college classrooms, and school teachers usually haven't taught in universities. Jo has worked in both worlds. She currently teaches landscape architecture at the University of Sheffield.

Martin Griffin has spent his career teaching in three different sixth form colleges. He has been a head of sixth form and a deputy head teacher, guiding and supporting young people with their university applications. He is currently an award-winning writer of both fiction and non-fiction, and he trains teachers to help students to perform at their best.

When you add it up, between us we've taught A levels for thirty years, alongside various side quests into GCSEs, evening classes and primary school workshops. And we've also been adult students a total of eight times between us, making mistakes along the way, so we still vividly remember what it's like to try to learn something new, deal with unfamiliar settings, figure out what the teacher expects and submit our work on time.

Most of all, we've helped sort out two careers' worth of students' problems. When you've been helping students for as long as we have, study-related issues become quite familiar. The same ones tend to crop up each year, and we've got better at advising students the longer we've done these jobs. This book is the outcome of that experience.

So welcome, travellers one and all, to *The Backpacker's Guide to University*.

Website: www.backpackersuni.com

BEFORE YOU TRAVEL

THE WAY OF THE BACKPACKER

University is a journey that can be travelled in different ways. The way in which you approach this adventure determines how much learning you will get out of it, and how much you enjoy it. Two people taking the same trip might say totally different things about the experience: one seeing the whole thing as an adventure; the other treating it as an endurance test. University is an investment of time, money and effort, and we would like to see you travel well.

SO WHY BE A BACKPACKER?

Backpackers are active explorers.

They take control of their own experiences and take responsibility for where they're going and how they're going to get there. They are creative and adaptable. This flexibility means they can take chances, build relationships and discover new and better ways of doing things. Backpackers solve problems, find joy in the journey and, above all, travel with intention.

Consider this book your guide to a unique and fascinating trip. We manage to sustain the backpacker metaphor pretty well throughout, though in places the prose creaks a little, like the timbers of a three-masted schooner in heavy seas off the Azores.

But we like the metaphor for a reason. We want to help you to see that good habits are important if you wish to have an enjoyable adventure in higher education. We don't think you should be relentlessly focused on the final degree classification that you might get, because that is a reductive approach and will mean missing out on all kinds of opportunities during this exciting stage of life. We don't want you to just 'survive' university, or to feel that your grades need to be better than everyone else's. Because we don't think that's what these years should be about.

Put simply, the backpacker approach means having a small number of useful techniques at the ready, taking the initiative and entering into a true spirit of adventure. In other words, get your travel plans in order, navigate your course and strap in for the ride!

HOW TO USE THIS BOOK

Read it in stages.

In an ideal world you would check through most of this book in the months before setting off. That way you would know what kinds of advice it contains, so you could easily dip into it whenever the need arises. But travel experiences rarely present us with an ideal world, and even though this is a short book, we know that you might not find the time. So, instead:

- Start reading Part One a couple of weeks before you go to uni and finish it a week or so into your course.
- Then start reading Part Two, aiming to complete it within the first two to three weeks of your course.
- Then briefly glance through Part Three, so that if you encounter rocky territory, you know where to turn for help! Don't dwell on this section now. It's for emergencies only.

In places we will ask you to briefly write notes, make plans or draw things, so it will be useful if you have a notebook or journal to hand.

WHAT IS A UNIVERSITY?

So what is this strange new landscape you'll be exploring?

For the purposes of this book, we'll say that university is an institution where research-led teaching takes place alongside the research itself.

'Research-led teaching' means teaching staff will often be actively con-ducting research or will practise as professionals in their area of speciality, which means you'll be spending time with experts who are prominent in their field. This could apply to a range of disciplines; you could be taught

4

by practising architects, artists, novelists or poets, medics, designers, lawyers, business people and so on.

Almost all UK universities are independent bodies with charitable status, so they are not run for profit. Many students will be undergraduates – meaning they are studying to gain their first degree or bachelor's.

You will hear phrases like 'Russell Group', 'The Sutton 30' and 'red brick' used to describe some universities. The first is a group of 24 institutions which between them win more than two-thirds of the research money given to UK universities.[1] Over three-quarters of a million students study at Russell Group universities, and they attract international students as they have an excellent reputation around the world.[2] The Sutton 30 is a list – created by social mobility charity The Sutton Trust – of the UK's 30 most prestigious and selective universities, used to measure how many students from poorer backgrounds attend year-on-year. 'Red brick' is a looser term which derives from the architecture of 'newer' universities, first used a little snootily by the Victorians to describe unis in six big industrial cities and now applied more broadly to many universities which were founded before the 1960s. Note that 'Oxbridge' is not a university. This is an embarrassing mistake to make.

In your first year, the key parts of the university that you'll need to learn your way around will be the building where your department is located, and maybe other buildings where you will be taught, the library for your subject area and the students' union, which exists for the students' welfare and enjoyment and will offer useful facilities and services. You might be living on or near campus, in university-owned accommodation, and you might make use of campus sports facilities.

WHAT IS UNIVERSITY FOR?

It's for many things, of course, but we want to simplify a little here.

Think of it as training for the journey that is the rest of your life. In preparing for that trip, uni will give you a wonderful grounding in three areas: *independence, innovation* and *expertise*. You won't get to explore these in the same way via any other route. It is true that other paths in life might teach you to be autonomous or to innovate, or might give you expertise: early parenthood, for example, or starting your own business straight out of school. You might have already done these things – if so, you will perhaps agree that it is a wonderful but tough way to learn. However, university provides a stable, guided and gradual framework, allowing you to develop these capabilities. And once you have them, you are more suited to a number of roles in professional, vocational and business life.

---

1   See https://www.russellgroup.ac.uk/who-we-are.
2   See https://www.russellgroup.ac.uk/who-we-are.

INDEPENDENCE

Graduates tend to find work that both allows and requires increasing levels of autonomy. Rather than having their time micromanaged, graduates are often expected to work independently or in teams without close guidance. You might be sequencing and organising your own work, deciding what your next priorities are, building teams of people to get something done, then feeding back your progress. Employers want graduates because they'll get on and do things without constant supervision. Of course, you might want to become a freelancer or start your own business and be truly independent.

INNOVATION

Graduates tend to find work that requires them to solve interesting problems. They're often paid to fix or improve the way things currently work or respond to change. Those who work in education design lessons and try to improve the ways in which their classrooms are run. Those in business seek efficiencies or new customers. Those in advertising are tasked with engaging consumers or changing people's behaviours. In short, employers want graduates because they're good at finding creative solutions to important problems. Many well-paid, responsible non-graduate jobs – being a train driver, for example – might be great career options, but the opportunities for independence and innovation will be minimal.

EXPERTISE

Graduates tend to find work that requires that they learn new things and demonstrate growing skills and knowledge. Some get work that requires them to use the expertise they gained at university – a working knowledge of chemistry, how the human body works or how to design and build something, for example. Some will use their transferable skills – because university has proved that they can read and understand new information quickly or dive deep into a topic and figure it out. Employers want graduates because they have subject-specific expertise, or because they know how to get it through their finely honed study skills.

Nobody is expecting all of this from you right now, however. You have the privilege of a few years of training and experimentation, with space to make mistakes and explore your strengths and weaknesses, before making those first job applications.

A BACKPACKER'S PHRASEBOOK

This is a world with its own, often confusing, language. Here are some handy terms that you are likely to find used frequently by the locals who you'll encounter on your journeys. Learn how to use them and you can hope to pass for someone who knows what they are doing. They are organised by theme.

YOUR CLASSES

Lecture – typically a non-interactive 'lesson', with a presentation from a subject expert, usually including slides, lasting for at least fifty minutes, and conducted in a lecture theatre which might seat anything from fifty to 350 people. Students are expected to listen and take notes, and often have an opportunity to ask questions at the end.

Seminar – a discussion-based session for a small group, perhaps six to ten students, led by an academic. You will need to do reading or other work to prepare for the seminar, and you will be expected to listen to others as well as make your own spoken contributions. There's nowhere to hide in a seminar – you will be asked questions, so you must do the preparation. Seminars could be among the richest learning experiences you'll ever have.

Workshop – this is likely to involve cooperative work with other students, completing set tasks with support from a tutor. This term is used quite broadly, so it may be a theory-based workshop, in which you tackle problems or scenarios, but in subjects with a practical element it could mean actually making or designing something or learning to use equipment. Obviously, 'workshop' could also mean a type of room.

Lab – short for laboratory. Similar to a workshop, but much more likely to be a hands-on learning session. Science students will likely have a lot of lab sessions on their timetable, when they conduct experiments in a laboratory. Some social science and design-based courses also use this word, just to confuse everybody.

Tutorial – typically a one-to-one meeting with your tutor to discuss your work: either something that you are currently working on or that you have previously submitted. Tutorials can also be conducted in small groups, perhaps with one tutor to three students, so that you can learn from advice given to your peers and see how others approach the assignment. Do listen to everyone!

YOUR TEACHERS AND PEERS

Professor – in the UK and Europe, professor is the title given to a senior academic, an expert in their field, who will be spending a lot of time doing their own research. Your contact with them is likely to be through lectures, which are a great opportunity to learn about the research work they do. Elsewhere, any academic teacher might be called 'professor'.

Academic – often used to mean any person who teaches in a university. They don't necessarily all do research, though many do.

Tutor – used flexibly to mean anybody employed by the university to teach you. This could include graduate teaching assistants (GTAs), who are usually PhD students who are doing some undergraduate teaching alongside their own research. It could also include professionals who usually work outside of the university but come in to teach specific modules or courses, perhaps one day a week. Your personal tutor is different; they are assigned to be your first point of contact for non-academic help and support.

Undergraduate – this is someone studying for their first degree, so they have not graduated yet.

Postgraduate – or postgrad – any student who already has their first undergraduate degree. Some are taught students, studying for a master's or a postgraduate diploma or certificate, for example, and some are researchers working towards a PhD.

DIVIDING UP TIME

Module – a chunk of your course that has its own learning objectives. A module usually runs for a term, or half term, and ends in an assessment, which will usually be some kind of exam or final piece of work. You are likely to be following more than one module, perhaps four of them, at a time, and will need to organise yourself.

Semester/term – you might be familiar with terms from school. Originating in the Christian calendar, there are three terms per academic year: from September to Christmas, from Christmas to Easter, and from

Easter to June, all with breaks in between. Semesters divide the academic year into two parts instead, with the first semester usually running from early October to February, with a break in December. Then it's straight into the second semester, with a break in March/April and ending around early June. Assessments can happen 'mid-term' or at the end of each semester.

Office hours – these are the times of the week when an academic will be in their office and available for students to drop by and ask for help with their work. Office hours might be quite limited, as staff could be part-time and will often be teaching, researching, in meetings or on study visits. Each academic's office hours arrangement could be different – some are happy with you dropping in whenever; others have sign-up lists. Their preference is usually indicated on their email signature and possibly on a piece of paper pinned to their office door. Make them feel useful by popping in to see them!

READING, WRITING AND ASSESSMENT

Academic journals – high-status academic magazines (often found online but the university library might have them in paper form too) which publish peer-reviewed research in very specific fields. Examples include *Weed Research*[1] or *Small*, the journal of nanotechnology.[2] They are useful for finding internationally significant and up-to-date research, but can be a tough read for a new undergrad.

Peer-reviewed – any published research that has been through a rigorous process of checking by other experts in the field. This is information you can trust more than Wikipedia or even BBC Bitesize, neither of which are to be cited as academic sources. Ever.

Plagiarism/unfair means – both these terms refer to cheating, perhaps by copying others' work, whether it be published or unpublished, and passing it off as your own by not crediting the authors. Your uni will have guidance on avoiding plagiarism on its website. Follow these rules. You also need to be fully aware of the rules about using AI in the course of your work. This will vary according to subject area, and quite possibly

---

1   See https://onlinelibrary.wiley.com/journal/13653180?msockid=
    20109158d16867ca24298464d02566aa.
2   See https://onlinelibrary.wiley.com/journal/16136829?msockid=
    20109158d16867ca24298464d02566aa.

from module to module, so you need to make sure that you know the rules, as cheating isn't tolerated, and you could be required to leave.

Summative feedback – feedback and final grades given on work submitted. You will likely be given a mark, a degree classification and written feedback to highlight the strengths and weaknesses in the work.

Formative feedback – feedback given throughout the module about how to improve your work before the final hand-in.

VLE – is a virtual learning environment. It's the go-to place for communication from your teachers. You will be given updates, resources and instructions via the VLE, and probably submit work here, too.

THE SETTING

Campus – the buildings and grounds of the university. Some are very clearly defined as a place, perhaps having a rural setting which holds all aspects of student life close together, like Keele University or Lancaster University. There are urban campuses too, like the University of Birmingham, where the uni buildings are set apart from the rest of the city. Some universities are dispersed over a wide area, but still have a campus-like feel in places because surrounding businesses cater very much to a student population – for example, on Manchester's Oxford Road.

Halls – this means student housing, and could refer to shared accommodation with catering and many individual bedrooms, shared flats owned by the university, and sometimes large apartment buildings which are privately owned, more expensive, and may have gyms, cafes and reception staff. Most students spend their first year of university living in halls.

Students' union – every university will have a students' union. The NUS – the National Union of Students – has a presence on every university campus. The union is an invaluable part of student life; it's a hub for socialising and welfare support.

One final note on vocabulary. In this book we are going to use the word 'teacher' when we want to refer generally to any person who teaches you, whether they be a GTA, tutor, lecturer, professor or anything else.

HOW IS STUDYING AT A
UNIVERSITY DIFFERENT?

Your previous experience of education, believe it or not, was pretty much like an all-inclusive trip. Bear with us on this. You might not have realised it when you were at school or college, but your teachers spent a great deal of time and energy on making sure you succeeded. While you got on and studied, they assigned target grades, sifted through coursework, gave feedback, monitored attendance and ran booster sessions. All of this meant that if there was a problem with your progress, your school or college probably spotted it. Your job was to get on with your work while others attended to the bigger picture.

University is different. This is not an all-inclusive package tour. Your tutors and lecturers are each employed to do different things. They're conducting research in their specific areas of expertise, running experiments, collecting data and publishing their findings in academic journals. They're applying for funding to run new research projects, or they're taking part in conferences where they present their work. The benefits of this come back to you, because their ever-growing expertise is your learning resource. They are doing all this while planning lectures, seminars and workshops, and giving you feedback.

But they haven't got time to sift through attendance or progress data and go looking for students who need extra support, because there are maybe a hundred students in that lecture theatre on a Tuesday morning, then another two hundred on a Thursday afternoon, and so on. They're ready and willing to help – but they're expecting you to come to them, and will be delighted when you do so.

So, your job isn't to wait for help anymore. You'll need to follow the way of the backpacker – and seek it out.

A final word on marking and grading. When you were at school or college, an exam board assessed and graded your final work. At university, each department marks its own students' work. Your professor *is* your final examiner, both teaching and assessing you – *so what they teach you is what they want to see in your work.* And the grading system at university is different. Gone are grades A, B, C and so on. Instead, you'll be awarded first class, commonly just called a first, for work that scores above 70%; upper second class, or a 2:1, for work that scores above 60%; lower second class, or a 2:2, for work that scores above 50%; and third class for work that scores above 40%.

CHOOSE YOUR OWN ADVENTURE

Before video games were really big, you could buy books which told a story that positioned the reader as the main character. They were adventures in which you could choose what you wanted to happen next by turning to a signposted page. It would go something like this ...

'You are standing in a clearing surrounded by tall trees. Ahead of you there is a leafy tunnel heading deep into the woods. In the distance you can hear the approach of thundering hooves. You remember that the local species of rhinoceros are renowned for their extreme aggression. Do you run for the tunnel (turn to page 13), climb the nearest tree (turn to page 29) or pick up a sharp stick from the ground and adopt a fighting stance (page 102)?'

The outcomes weren't always predictable, and there tended to be more than one 'right' answer, but you knew that there were better and worse choices to make. So it is with this adventure right now.

Like a choose your own adventure, you don't need to read this book in the order we have written it. To see how that might work, try one or all of these routes through:

- ▣ If you want a journey in which clear mental focus on your studies is going to be your top priority, take a short hop to **ACTIVITY 1.7** on page 43, **ACTIVITY 1.9** on page 55 and **ACTIVITY 2.8** on page 105, where you will see activities to help you achieve this.

- ▣ If you want your uni experience to be about making good connections with others, try jumping ahead to Passport Stamp – Try a New Sport on page 17, **ACTIVITY 1.10** on page 59 and **ACTIVITY 2.5** on page 91, which will offer some support.

■ Perhaps you reckon that your own shaky self-belief might hold you back in having a successful experience? If so, go directly to **ACTIVITY 1.3** on page 31, **ACTIVITY 1.5** on page 39 and **ACTIVITY 2.7** on page 97.

We promise that none of these pages will read, 'You have been trampled by rhinoceroses. You are dead.'

PASSPORT STAMPS – STEPPING INTO YOUR NEW SOCIAL LIFE

Perhaps you've seen those beautiful micro-artworks that are passport stamps. When passing through border control and having your passport checked by an actual person rather than a machine, you sometimes get an inked rubber stamp thwacked down onto a page of your passport, leaving a beautiful memento of your visit. They're not something you can buy – like a souvenir from a tourist tat shop – you have to be there, crossing that border, taking that next adventurous step.

In ten different places in this book, you will find our university-specific passport stamps. They are marked with the passport symbol you see above. Each one is designed to encourage you to take a step into the unknown, by doing something sociable that you have not done before – to collect that metaphorical stamp. To guide you, each one clearly states the intention behind taking that action. And each has a prompt for you to reflect on how you felt taking that step: what worked and what didn't, and whether you'd like to step any further in that direction.

The passport stamps aren't just there for the fun of it. Good mental health comes from making connections with people, experiencing a sense of community, taking part and feeling like you belong. Starting university certainly provides one of the best opportunities of your life to try new things, make friends and have different experiences. Have a go. Because if you don't try things, you might never try that one thing that turns out to be really important for *you*.

If you would like to look at all the passport stamps now, see pages 17, 29, 38, 52, 58, 64, 78, 103, 108 and 119.

The first challenge is on page 17, and it's a good one to do early on, before teaching starts. During freshers' week, all the societies are likely to be recruiting new members, so be on the lookout for groups to join.

PASSPORT STAMP –
TRY A NEW SPORT

Intention – be fit, make friends, have a laugh – all of which are good for your mental health.

Action – right at the start of the new academic year, sign up to a sports club. It doesn't have to be something you've done before, but think instead about whether you are broadly suited to the demands of the sport and to the level of seriousness of that club. Crucially, you then need to actually turn up to practice sessions, matches and related socials. Do this for a few weeks. You need to try for this long to properly explore whether this club could be for you.

Reflection – after those few weeks, ask yourself: have you met people you like? Were they welcoming? Did you have fun? If you answer yes to all these, it's a no-brainer – keep going. It *really* doesn't matter whether you are any good at the sport; this isn't about getting to the next Olympics. If you felt like a fish out of water, don't give up, try a different club. If you sometimes struggle with social situations, sport can be a more structured way of interacting with people and helping to feel that you belong. It gives you common ground to talk about, and all those post-exercise endorphins will do you nothing but good, boosting your mood no end.

PART ONE
SETTING OUT

Part One is all about getting ready for your journey through academia, with mental preparations and practical tasks to help set you up for the ride of your life.

In this section, we offer twelve activities to do before you arrive, and in those early days at university. We've chosen them carefully because they're important things to get sorted if you are to start as you mean to go on. You might not feel that you need to complete them all, but read each one carefully and give it some time and thought.

THE TOURIST VERSUS THE BACKPACKER – STARTING WITH THE RIGHT MINDSET

How do you intend to conduct this once-in-a-lifetime trip?

Let's consider two distinct approaches:

1 **The Tourist.** Tourists are passive. Tourists hang out by the pool or pass by the sights of the city on an open-top bus. The tourist's default position is to wait for attention: wait until the tour guide sends the plan for the day, and expect the resort staff to bring that cold drink.

2 **The Backpacker.** Backpackers are active participants in the journeys they take. It means they're working harder than tourists – carrying their packs, travelling on foot, relishing the unfamiliar. They're nimble adventurers, curious and self-sufficient. The backpacker's default position is to seek. They find rich experiences. They do stuff.

Choosing the way of the backpacker will help you to immerse yourself in your uni experience, and give you rewards that can't be underestimated. Your teachers will be expecting proactive students who act as partners in learning. By taking on this identity before you set out, you'll travel with a sense of agency and responsibility as you fully explore the exciting opportunities around you.

TASK

The way you define yourself – tourist or backpacker – will determine how you respond to changing circumstances. Consider the following scenarios and reflect on how you would act in each. In your notebook, draw out a simple scale like this one:

TOURIST   BACKPACKER

And remember, these are all scenarios that will absolutely happen at some point!

Scenario – a lecturer delivers a compelling exploration of their topic, moving quickly through some big, unfamiliar ideas, leaving you slightly confused.

The Tourist	The Backpacker
Keeps their head down, doesn't make eye-contact and prays they don't get asked a question.	Asks an open question at the end of the presentation, looking for clarity.
Waits for someone to notice they're struggling and offer additional help and attention.	Waits behind to ask for a reading recommendation.
Complains about the staff to their friends afterwards.	Checks in with another student, curious to see if they understood the topic a little better.
Tries to put it out of their mind.	Spends half an hour in the library afterwards, researching some of the key terms discussed.
Makes a private decision to skip the lecture next time that teacher is delivering.	Accesses the presentation on the VLE afterwards to go over it again.

Think about what kind of learner you have been: the old you. Where would you put that person on the scale? Where would you like your new you to be going forward? And finally, where could the best you aspire to be?

Reflect on these questions and make your three marks – for old you, new you and best you – on the scale in your notebook.

Now do the same for the next two scenarios.

Scenario – you get feedback for an assessed piece of work and your mark is unexpectedly low.

The Tourist	The Backpacker
Dismisses it as an error on the part of the marker – 'They just don't get me!' Tries to explain it away or minimise it – 'I was tired/hungover/ill.' 'I missed a key lecture.' 'I don't care, it wasn't a big proportion of the marks for the semester.' Is so wounded by the experience that they are stunned into inactivity. Puts it out of their minds, deletes or hides the feedback and gets on with the next thing.	Asks for more feedback about where they went wrong. Takes it seriously, but not as a personal attack. Makes an honest assessment of their levels of effort and engagement, and adjusts accordingly. Makes a plan to improve, perhaps even to resubmit the work.

Scenario – a lecturer advertises an interesting extracurricular activity – perhaps a competition, a study trip or the opportunity to take part in a research project.

The Tourist	The Backpacker
Considers the possible disruption to their comfort.	Investigates further, curious to see if it might be for them.
Thinks about the extra work which might disturb their life of ease.	Thinks about the new people they might meet along the way.
Imagines the hassle associated with filling out the application form, getting travel insurance or attending an extra meeting or two.	Imagines the new experiences which might emerge, and the learning opportunities that come with them.
Wonders why it's worth bothering, since it doesn't have any impact on their final grade.	Persuades a friend to join them to find out more, asks around to see if others have done it, or energises a group to take part.
Can't understand why anyone would volunteer to do 'extra work'.	Develops a stronger connection to their community.

The closer to the backpacker end of the scale you can get, the more you'll enjoy university, meet interesting people and have exciting things happen in your life. It's that important.

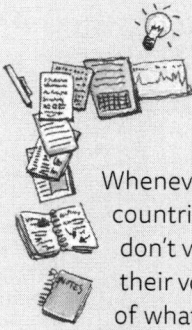

RESEARCH CORNER – MAKE POSITIVE BEHAVIOURS PART OF YOUR IDENTITY

Whenever elections come around in democratically run countries, a proportion of people who are eligible to do so don't vote. There are many reasons for this. They may feel their vote will make no difference, or they may be ignorant of what different political parties offer and feel they lack the expertise to make a choice.

Attempts are often made to encourage greater voter participation. In one interesting study, the aim was to increase a person's likelihood of voting by changing the language they used to describe themselves (Bryan et al., 2011). Some were asked to think of themselves as 'a voter', as if the process of voting were part of their identity. It's just who they are. Others were asked to commit to an action – to go and vote.

Which group was more likely to take part in the process? Well, 95.5% of those who were asked to think of themselves as voters went to the ballot box. And of those who were urged to complete an action – to go and vote – 81.8% turned out (Bryan et al., 2011, p. 12654). That's a significant difference.

You can see this effect all around you. If you regularly refer to yourself as 'a runner', you're much more likely to lace up your trainers and hit the road. If you think of yourself as 'a healthy eater', you're less likely to expend mental energy considering that huge slice of cake. If you mentally label yourself 'a team player', you're much more likely to cooperate with others or join a study group.

You can use these findings to your advantage. If you want to change your behaviour, start by changing the way you describe yourself. You're a backpacker, not a tourist!

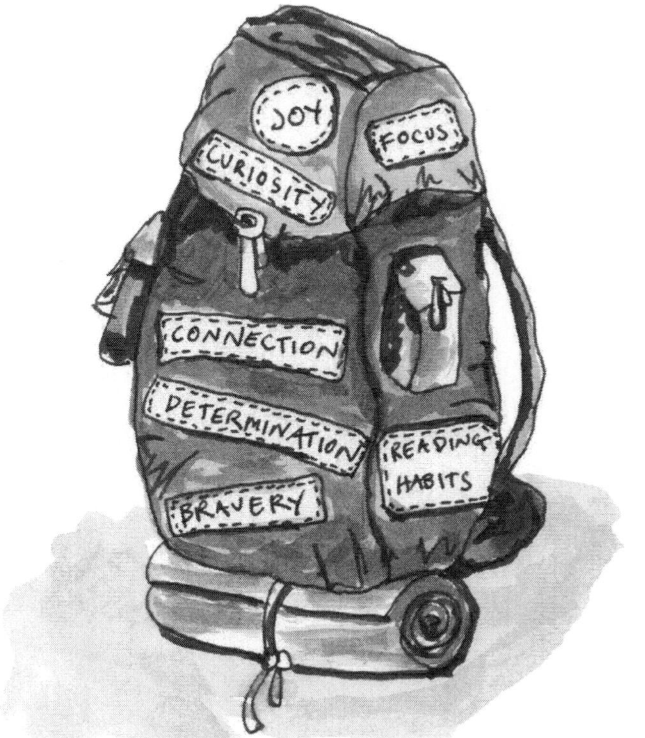
JOY
FOCUS
CURIOSITY
CONNECTION
DETERMINATION
READING HABITS
BRAVERY

THE PACKING LIST – CONSIDERING THE CULTURE YOU'RE LEAVING BEHIND

Do you remember what it was like to move from primary school to high school, or from education to employment? At some point, you will have had to make a big adjustment from one working culture to another.

In his book *Hell Yeah or No*, Derek Sivers (2020) writes about how to manage personal change. He offers the idea that just as a fish doesn't know that it is in water, because that is its only experience of the world, people are so fully immersed in the culture that surrounds them, they can't easily see beyond it (Sivers, 2020, p. 23). When you first start university, it's the same thing. You will have been a part of your previous working environment and you'll have got used to it. You know what the values are, how they play out and what people expect of you.

Sivers recommends taking small actions that start you on a path to changing your self-perception. In this exercise, we ask you to reflect on the culture in your previous environment, to think about how it shaped you, what your behaviours were like and what you want to leave behind.

TASK

We suggest you take two small steps towards your new working culture.

Step 1 – open your notebook and scribble down some reflections on your most recent working culture. Be as honest as you can, then think about what you can learn:

▇ In your previous learning culture, did you usually feel stretched and challenged to do your best work?

▇ Did you sometimes feel uncomfortably stretched? (If so, that is usual for many learners.)

▇ Did you challenge yourself to do better or rely on others to motivate you?

- Did you make the best possible use of your work time?
- How focused were you on your tasks? Were you ever off-task or distracted?
- What skills did you learn? What skills did you hope to learn, but didn't?
- Did you feel enthusiasm for your work? Was this because of the culture or despite it?
- What were your most helpful work habits, and how were you supported in these?
- What were your least helpful habits, and why did they become habitual?
- Did your peers raise your game or lower your standards?
- Did you believe you could succeed in your work? Why, or why not?
- Imagine you are going to spend an extra two years staying in the same place, doing the same things. How does that feel? What would be missing? Is it time for change?

Step 2 – summarise your thoughts from the above exercise by making a short packing list that will help you to take the right things with you on your university journey, such as enthusiasm, optimism and curiosity.

Among the students on your new course, there will be people who have very effective working habits, because they come from supportive learning cultures. There will be others who need to leave behind destructive, damaging or ineffective learning cultures. There will be those who come from backgrounds where learning just wasn't valued or understood, but who managed to secure their university place despite this.

Do any of these descriptions match you? What habits and characteristics will you take with you to university and what will you leave behind? Be honest with yourself and take time to reflect.

And, as one final reflection on your packing list, make sure you truly intend to leave those unhelpful things behind. Don't accidentally pack your procrastination – leave no space for stowaways!

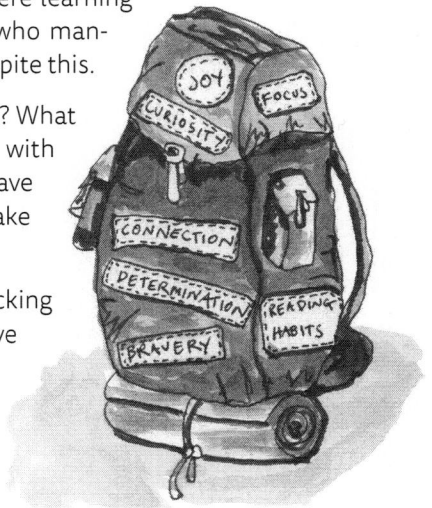

PASSPORT STAMP – CONTROL YOUR BUDGET

Intention – have a budget and stick to it.

Action – if you've never had a monthly budget before, here's what to do. Ideally you should set up a spreadsheet or use an app built for student finance,[1] you could just make a table in a Word document or even write it down in the back of a notebook.

If you are starting from scratch, remember that the aim is to be aware of how much money you have available to spend each month (or week, if it's easier) and how much you will need to pay for your essentials. The amount you have left over is your disposable income.

Your *income* could be from a grant, loan, earnings, benefits or, if you are lucky, parental contributions or a scholarship.

Your *essential expenditure* will depend on what type of accommodation you have. If you're in halls, you'll have most of your bills covered. Once you're renting your own place, you'll be thinking about rent, as well as water and power bills. Remember that students are exempt from paying council tax. Wherever you're living, you'll need to set aside money for food, transport, phone, Wi-Fi, clothing, and contents insurance to cover your personal possessions (possibly paid yearly or termly). Depending on your course, you might need to budget for books, equipment and study visits. You'll probably also need to factor in a deposit of a few hundred pounds on your room/flat/house, which you'll get back at the end of the year, provided you have left it in a good state. We recall once losing a proportion of the deposit because the skirting boards hadn't been dusted, so watch out for this kind of nonsense from landlords and letting agents – leave it pristine! Check the inventory on the day you move in so that you can make it clear, in writing, if anything was broken, worn or damaged before you took over the tenancy.

So, just list all the amounts in two columns – incomings and outgoings – then add up the individual items and take your expenditure

---

1   For example, see https://www.timeshighereducation.com/student/advice/top-phone-apps-managing-student-finance.

away from your income. It's worth itemising things separately so you can easily go back and make adjustments if any of the costs change or you need to find ways to make savings.

Reflection – hopefully you're left with a positive number! Ideally this will be enough to cover your hobbies and social life. Don't be too surprised if this number is very small, or a minus. If you need to boost your income, consider what part-time work you could do. Sometimes paid work can be a real joy, so don't see this necessarily as a bad thing. Bar and restaurant jobs, for example, can be very sociable and you might get good tips, though the hours will be late so you shouldn't overstretch yourself by doing too many nights per week. Perhaps you can even get work in line with your academic or career interests, which will enhance your CV and be a good learning experience.

It's very important, and well within your capabilities, to get on top of financial matters from the start, so this doesn't become a source of anxiety. If in doubt over financial matters, your students' union may well offer guidance and help, but you can also try the ever-useful moneysavingexpert.com, which is independent and full of links and advice.

THE FRESH START – COMMITTING TO NEW BEHAVIOURS

Imagine it's welcome week and you're at university – a place that might as well be a foreign country. You're wondering whether you should eat the food from 'that' van, and what might be the best response to the question 'Are you a fresher?' You're surrounded by new faces, new places, new ways of doing things. No one knows you. Perhaps you think you're going to have to prove yourself all over again.

This isn't bad news, though. A fresh start is a chance for reinvention.

If you want to set new expectations for yourself but aren't sure where to start, consider the approach of artist and writer of best-selling books on creativity Austin Kleon. He sets high standards for himself in terms of a daily dedication to his work, and captures them as simply expressed standards he tries to hold himself to. Some of his include:

- Don't be afraid of sharing your work. For Kleon, that means writing a poem and posting it online every single day: 'Most days they're mediocre, some days they're great, and some days they're awful.'

- Use pockets of time to work in the day wherever possible: 'You find time the same place you find spare change: in the nooks and crannies ... between the big stuff – your commute, your lunch break.'

- Twice a week, get up early and work on something that matters to you because: '... building a body of work is all about the slow accumulation of effort over time.' (Kleon, 2013)

TASK

Choose three things you want to form the basis of your fresh start.

Like Kleon, keep them simple, memorable and relevant to your work. We've given you a dozen to start with – added to Kleon's three, that's fifteen in total for you to consider. They might not all suit you, so throw out the ones which seem too cheesy, but examine each one carefully before selecting your own top three:

- Build good relationships with others.
- Contribute something useful to the community.
- Help out others when you can, and ask for help when you need it.
- Be positive and imaginative.
- Don't place limits on what you can achieve.
- Be curious and ask questions.
- Enjoy every possible moment.
- Change your mind.
- Read more.
- If there's an interesting opportunity, take it.
- See the best in others.
- Make mistakes, learn and move on.

Make a note of them in your notebook.

RESEARCH CORNER – THE POWER OF NEW BEGINNINGS

Often it can feel hard to change our behaviours, particularly if comfortable habits have established themselves over time. It's a very human thing to try to change but then fail.

One interesting piece of research suggests that goal-motivation – how committed we feel to changing our behaviour and embracing a fresh start – can often be much stronger if we attach some importance to the day we begin (Dai et al., 2015).

In one study, participants were asked to set themselves a goal. Every participant chose something personal to them: something they really wanted to change about themselves, such as their levels of organisation or the amount of effort they put into their studies.

One group were assigned a start date for their new goal: *March 20th.*

The other group were given the same start date, but it was expressed as: *March 20th – the first day of spring.*

Which group showed higher levels of goal-motivation? The participants who were given this extra information. Suddenly, the start day was powerful, important and loaded with positive meaning.

You can do this too. If you're trying to change the way you approach work, instead of just choosing a random date in the near future and hoping for the best, find a way of attaching meaning to the date. It could be … the first day of a season, the first day of a semester, the tenth day of term, a half-birthday, a parent's or sibling's birthday, an important day in history …

If you find a way of making the date meaningful, you're much more likely to make change stick.

QUIET DESK

THIRD FLOOR

STUDY BOOTHS

GROUP WORKING

SECOND FLOOR

COMFY SEATS NEAR WINDOW

SUBJECT BOOKSHELVES

FIRST FLOOR

MAGAZINES + JOURNALS

CAFE

BIG TABLES

GROUND FLOOR

THREE STEPS AHEAD – HOW TO SCOPE OUT NEW TERRITORY

You may have used travel guides when planning a holiday. You can flick through their pages and they'll tell you about the place you're planning to visit – its culture and currency, the local customs, the lie of the land, the top attractions, and so on.

University is no different. Before you go, spend some time scrolling the website to get a sense of what your new home will be like. You can have a look at the campus map, check staff lists to see who could be teaching you or figure out where the gym and swimming pool are.

Once you've done all that, you'll probably be keen to have a look at details of your modules, and teaching staff, but you won't have access to these until you have enrolled. As soon as you have, here are three things to scope out.

TASK

THE VLE

This stands for virtual learning environment, a phrase so lacking in allure that it is usually replaced by a brand name: Moodle, Blackboard or Ultra. Universities use these as a go-to place for resources and communications, keeping everyone up to date with what's happening.

Almost all of your instructions and assignments for each module will be here. There will probably be a teaching schedule, learning aims and submission requirements, and your reading list, as well as signposts to other useful resources. Get into the habit of regularly checking the pages for each module. There may well be a different tab for every week. For many courses, it is likely that you will have to submit work through this platform, and you will probably receive your results and feedback here too.

Your task is simple: just set yourself a reminder on your calendar to check in with the VLE at the same time every day – for example, at 6 pm – so you know what to expect the following day. We also recommend that you read the submission requirements and learning objectives carefully at the start of the module so that you know what you are aiming for, otherwise how will you know how to focus your efforts? Think of the VLE as your official guide to all the essentials, because, without it, it is possible to take a wrong turn.

THE READING LIST

In all honesty, different teaching staff will have different approaches to reading lists. Some will be very long, and the tutors will genuinely intend (hope) for you to read all the items. Others will be extensive, but you are expected to treat them more like a long list to select from, perhaps following your own interests. Some will be shorter, select lists of compulsory reading, perhaps with tasks to complete, such as questions to answer as you go. Some modules might have set reading each week, which may be to help you with an assignment or essential preparation for a seminar.

Your task is in two parts:

1   Have a look at your reading list and interpret the intentions behind it. Is it all essential reading? It will perhaps be clear, or it might be more mysterious, in which case you should tactfully ask the module leader about their intentions (by email or after a lecture).

2   Once you have that straight, use the list to set out your own personal reading schedule (for advice about schedules see **ACTIVITY 1.11** on page 65). Put it in your diary, calendar or planner. If it is already laid out on the VLE week-by-week, your job is done – just remember to set aside enough time to do it, checking ahead of time to see how long the reading is and what the level of challenge is – both may vary. If your list is non-essential, be selective. It is important to keep your plans realistic. Ask for help with anything you are finding hard, from a tutor or a study group meeting. Enjoy the feeling of ticking the readings off your list one by one!

THE LIBRARY

Some of the items on your reading list will be print books and journals, but most are likely to be e-books or papers that you can find online. Either way, these items will often be held in some form by the university library. There could well be several libraries, each catering to different subject areas. You will be able to track down anything you need using the search facility on the library website. With electronic resources, you can read them online or download a PDF. With paper-based items, you'll need to check whether it is in stock, and its location, note down the library number (which will appear on the spine) and set off to find it on foot. The great thing about using the library's physical resources is that you can browse the shelves relevant to you and find unexpected treasures in the form of books that your peers, and perhaps even your tutors, haven't read. In addition, the library is an excellent place to work, with its different types of study zones – some set aside for silent work and others for group work or meetings.

Your task is to visit the library just after it opens one morning. Take a walk around and try to find your ideal working environment: maybe you'd like a comfier chair, a good view from the window, an isolated spot with no one else around, somewhere with a background buzz of chatter, or a desk right next to the shelves for your subject? Take a seat, choose something from your reading list and get to work, consciously choosing to move to a different place if you find that your concentration is poor. Repeat until you find the sweet spot. It might be in a subject area completely different from your own, where you won't bump into anyone to distract you. If you have a regular favourite spot, you won't even have to think about the choice in future. Settle in and think about what a luxury it is to have somebody make you a reading list, and to have such a facility dedicated to helping you read it all.

For more advice on academic reading, see **ACTIVITY 2.1** on page 75.

Of course, you shouldn't avoid company all the time ...

PASSPORT STAMP – SPEAK TO STRANGERS

Intention – practise getting to know people and start to make new friends.

Action – chat to as many strangers as possible during the course of the first few weeks of the academic year. This includes people waiting for lectures to start, leaving taught sessions, queuing in the cafe, at your student accommodation, waiting at bus stops, and going to clubs and societies. Just not when they are trying to work in the library! Don't pre-judge people based on appearances, and remember that they won't be strangers for long. The main thing to remember is to keep these conversations light at first and not to go on at great length about your own life and interests. Ask them about themselves, but not in a creepy way. Don't hit on people. It's too soon. Be respectful and don't take it personally if people aren't up for a chat at that moment. Keep going until you've found some people you really like – or maybe never stop being approachable – as this is a brilliant life skill to have.

Reflection – did you enter into the spirit of it? If not, it's never too late, so just start afresh at any time. How many people did you talk to? Did it matter what you talked about? How could you go from that initial small talk to something with a bit more depth? Did you find some common ground? While differences can be good, it's hard to develop solid friendships if you don't have anything in common, or if you are opposed to each other's attitudes to life. Before you go much further, explore whether you are a good fit with these new folk. Trust your instincts and avoid people or groups who make you feel like a less good version of yourself. This includes groups based around shared addictions or other self-destructive behaviours. Look for people who seem to be enjoying life, interested in their work and seeding happiness around them.

One last thing: remember to keep in touch with your old friends. You don't have to cut ties with your pre-uni network. If you feel lonely, give a friend a call and actually hear their voice. If you want to check that they are OK, speak to them and have a proper catch-up, because it's very easy to miss emotional nuance in text messages.

ONE TICKET AT A TIME – HOW TO START GOOD HABITS NOW

In the popular BBC TV series *Race Across the World*, teams compete to cross a huge distance – for example, from the west coast to the east coast of Canada – on a tight budget and without mobile phones or internet access.

Such a journey might feel incredibly daunting, but the contestants stop at checkpoints along the way, travelling by any route and any means they like. They don't know what the ultimate destination will be, so they just take a leap of faith and tackle one leg of the journey at a time, planning as best they can, trusting in the process and committing to it.

If you've made a packing list full of good intentions, but the scope of your new student life seems quite a big challenge, remember that your university adventure is not going to be a single big-push epic voyage across a vast open ocean; it will happen in stages. And you will put ashore in many interesting ports along the way, travelling one ticket at a time towards your ultimate destination.

TASK

Consider the following suggestions for tickets you might use, one at a time:

■ **Ticket to Read** – if you are not a habitual reader but need to become one, take one book out of the library, read the relevant chapters and make notes as you go. Repeat.

■ **Ticket to Challenge** – if you're afraid that you lack some subject knowledge that your peers will already have, find an online lecture about the topic. Watch it, pressing pause and making notes as you go. You might still not fully understand it, but you will have progressed.

■ **Ticket to Talk** – if you think you might be coasting along without reaching your potential, find one person in your class who you think might be progressing more quickly than you. (There might be many to choose from – which is entirely normal!) Strike up a conversation about work. Sustain that conversation for as long as seems socially acceptable. If you are not a good judge of how long this might be, as a guide, stick to ten minutes. Listen to the ideas they bring to the conversation, and the way they express themselves – there will be things you can learn!

■ **The Dolly Parton Ticket** – if you have a habit of wasting time, make yourself a study timetable for a whole day, working 9 to 5, as Dolly says, breaking the day up into one-hour slots with an aim to be achieved in each. Have one hour for lunch. Stick to the plan. Repeat.

ACTIVITY 1.6
MAKE AN ITINERARY – PLOTTING THE SHAPE OF THE TERM AHEAD

An itinerary is a list of all the stopping-off points on your journey as you travel to your final destination. In mediaeval times, before maps were easy to come by, this was the way to get around, by asking for directions to the next town as you went along. Itineraries are good for people who prefer to plan, providing a clear structure for the times ahead so you can see what happens when.

TASK

A basic wall chart is what is needed here: either a physical one on a big bit of paper that you can display above your desk or an app that does the same thing. Have a look at our low-tech example, on page 42, which shows an imaginary autumn term.

Mark yours up with these things, in this order:

1   Exam dates and submission deadlines (these can't be changed unless you are ill and have supplied a doctor's note).

2   The days of work that you estimate you will need to prepare for those deadlines.

3   Time you can set aside for advance preparation for the next module.

4   Weekly wider reading time to broaden your knowledge.

5   Regular study group meeting time.

6   Any regular non-study commitments that you have, like sports practices and matches, drama group, volunteering and so on.

These are all the stops you have to make on your way through the term. The main point of this is to consolidate all the different demands on your time into one place, visually, so you can easily see where you are and what lies ahead. This should help you to keep on top of things. It also allows you to schedule the fun stuff for when you know you will have free time, or to spontaneously do fun stuff because you know that big deadline is still three weeks away!

| SUBMISSION DEADLINES | ▲ SPORT | ✦ STUDY GROUP | ◎ READING TIME | ⁺⁺⁺ DEADLINE PREP |

MAP YOUR WORKSPACES
– WHERE TO GO TO WORK

1 MAIN LECTURE HALL

2 SPORTS HUB

3 BOOKSHOP/ CAFE

4 TASTY CHEAP EATS

5 PARK / COFFEE HUT

6 PUBLIC LIBRARY

Arriving on campus is exciting and daunting at the same time.

In this exercise, you will explore and map the area around where you live and around your campus (these might be the same places if you live on campus, of course). The aim is to scope out the places where you will spend your working week. This is a great activity to do in the first term at university, because it supports you in feeling more at home in your new environment. It also helps you to frame that place as somewhere where you will enjoy doing daily productive work. You could do this exercise on your own or with a new acquaintance/future friend. The point is not to help you remember how to navigate your way around, but to remind you of all the options you have that can support your focus on various kinds of work.

TASK

Get yourself a map, print-out, screenshot or phone map. You could even just start with your notebook and a pen. The map needs to cover an area that is walkable from side to side in under 20 minutes.

Go on a tour of the local area, marking on your map, with a dropped pin or a note, the locations of useful places:

- The university library for your subject (note where the silent study areas are).
- The local public libraries.
- Bookable group workspaces (these might be in the library).
- Computer rooms for students – there will be many of these and you might not have to stick to the ones that are dedicated to your course.
- Quiet cafes where people are working on laptops.
- Noisy cafes where you could work with your headphones on.
- Comfortable shady benches where you could work outdoors in good weather (nowhere isolated, consider personal safety).
- Practical workshops/rehearsal spaces/studios/labs.
- Key buildings for your taught sessions.
- Places to go to during the day to reward yourself for hard work, like sports facilities, cafes for a cheap lunch, places where you will run into friends for a chat or green spaces to go for a walk.

If you want to go one step further, you could rate each of these locations for things like affordability, free Wi-Fi, possible distractions and so on. It might take a few tours to find and record all the best places, but this is a pleasure to do and time very well spent. You could soon be the person on your course who knows where everything is, whom others ask for help. Don't be the student who waits in the corridor for an hour between taught sessions, doom-scrolling and getting nothing done – this has neither academic nor social value.

In his book *How to Win at College*, Professor Cal Newport suggests finding a 'secret' study space where you know that interruptions will be zero – your friends won't walk past and stop to chat, there are no screens and it's really quiet. 'My secret study space was a little-used carrel at the end of a dimly lit, non-windowed book aisle,' he says, 'sitting at the end of a dark passage ... in complete silence, I found that I could work for hours with stunning concentration' (Newport, 2005, p. 172). He acknowledges, though, that using only this one workplace would end up too samey, so variety is important.

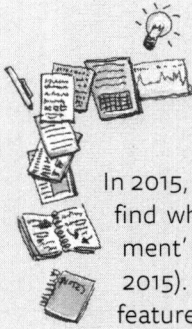

RESEARCH CORNER – ENVIRONMENT MATTERS

In 2015, academics from the University of Salford set out to find whether what they called the 'school built environment' has an impact on students' learning (Barrett et al., 2015). Large data sets were collected about the physical features of 153 teaching spaces across the UK, including things like lighting, heating, orientation, sound ... even colour choices in the interior design. Each of these factors was given a score out of five based on hard measurements and meter readings, and questionnaires collected perceptions from nearly four thousand students. Students' scores on national curriculum tests were also taken into account, to see if the rooms they had studied in might have had an impact on their performance.

What did they find? Here are the top three insights (Barrett et al., p. 127):

1   Up to 21% of students' progress could be linked to the quality of the light they work in. So you're looking for spaces with good levels of light: clear brightness that stimulates the eye without any glare.

2   Up to 17% of students' progress could be linked to the flexibility, openness and organisation of the space they work in. So look for space to spread out your work, to shift position, to move books and resources around on the desk in front of you so you can form a visual overview of the material.

3   Up to 16% of students' progress could be linked to the quality of the ventilation in their learning environment. So look for spaces with easy access to clean cool air. You ideally want somewhere well-ventilated and open feeling.

So where you choose to study will have an impact on your focus, your concentration and even your grade. Remember that as you put your workplace map together.

SETTLING INTO YOUR QUARTERS – HOW TO GET YOUR PERSONAL SPACE RIGHT

Sometimes your workplace won't quite measure up to the ideal, but a few tweaks could make it significantly better. Everyone has different preferences for their surroundings. Some may feel they can't travel without their collection of interesting pinecones, while others will need to instigate a clear-desk policy every night. Some backpackers might be struggling with a workspace that is really holding them back and need to bail out. So take some time to review your space …

Think about what you can see and hear from your desk. For example, if you have frequently noisy neighbours you may need to work elsewhere. If you like to work in cafes, you might want to have headphones with you in case of distractions. You could have a playlist of instrumental music or recordings of natural sounds, as you don't want to find yourself listening to your favourite artist instead of actually working. Don't depend on headphones too much though, as it's good to have the skill of tuning out background noise.

If your base camp looks out onto an uninspiring car park or a blank white wall, you could arrange a display of visual cues that support you when you are summoning up your powers of determination or creativity. Photos, postcards, doodles, maps, cards from friends – use whatever will keep you sharp, motivated and awake!

Remember that your desk (and you will need one) has just one purpose, so do everything you can to make sure that it doesn't double up as a dining table, board games arena or general clutter station. We promise that it will make a difference.

TASK

WORKSPACE AUDIT - FIVE-MINUTE CHECK

This activity is practical, not theoretical. Get your notebook and a pen, stand in your workspace and score your setup. Remember that you might need to work here for several hours at a time.

You'll be scoring each category in the table that follows out of 10 – with 0 being the least and 10 being the most – and jotting down the numbers in your notebook.

In the positives column, for example, a very comfy desk and chair would score a 10, but a room that is way too cold or too hot might only score a 2.

In the negatives column, a noisy room might score an 8 or more, but a silent room would be a zero. Constant interruptions from friends would be a 10, but your housemate bringing you a cuppa once a day could just be a 1.

Positives	Score	Negatives	Score
Comfortable desk and chair?		How problematic is the noise?	
Books/other resources within reach?		How crowded is the desk?	
Good Wi-Fi?		How much distraction from others?	
Pleasant lighting?		How many interruptions from tech?	
Comfortable temperature?		Danger of nodding off?	
Positive atmosphere?		Other irritants?	
Positives total		*Negatives total*	
Final total (positive total minus negative total)			

How did you do?

More than 40 – good stuff, you are either very lucky in your work environment or you've done a great job in setting yourself up for productive work. Consider tweaking anything that has reduced your score – could you add a bookshelf, or a small heater or fan, for example?

Between 30 and 39 – not too bad at all – but some tweaks may be needed. Could you get a more comfortable chair, have a serious tidy up and stick a 'do not disturb' sign on the door?

Between 20 and 29 – you may have a problem if you spend all your time here. Have you switched your phone notifications off and put your phone out of sight? Can you buy a cheap second-hand desk? If there are too many problems to fix, maybe you should reconsider where you work, and try some changes of scene.

Below 19 – this isn't going to work. If your home environment prevents you from working, you should use student workspaces provided by the university or look for another solution.

THE TRAVELLING LEARNER

Studies show that your recall of information can be improved by changing the physical context in which you work. It makes sense, if you find yourself easily bored or distracted by your environment, to move around during the day to refresh your mood. It is also true that sometimes you will encounter noisy building work nearby, or a Wi-Fi failure, or broken heating systems. In all these cases you'll need to use different venues for different occasions and perhaps even for different types of tasks. And, let's be honest, sometimes you need to escape to somewhere your friends or flatmates won't find you, because you need to focus 100%. Have some back-up workplaces in mind so that you can shift location at the drop of a hat (or Wi-Fi network)!

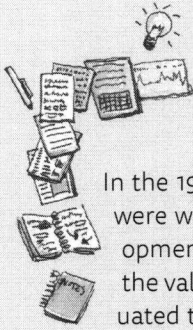

RESEARCH CORNER – THE POWER OF PERSONAL STUDY SPACES

In the 1980s two academics, Tom DeMarco and Tim Lister, were working in the fast-growing world of software development. This was a time when people were more aware of the value of concentration, because they weren't so habituated to constant distractions from technology. Intent on exploring what made some computer programmers more successful than others, they set up a huge coding tournament, inviting software companies to put forward their best programmers to solve a fiendish problem. The winners would get a prize and everyone else would get a full report detailing where they came in the pecking order – useful for companies who wanted to figure out what their competitors were up to.

Hundreds of entries came in, and the researchers began sifting through the results. Even though the best work was ten times more successful than the worst, they struggled to find any patterns. There was no connection between salary and success. There was no connection between time spent and success – in fact, the most successful entries were completed among the quickest. And there was no connection between experience and success. Coders with ten years' experience were doing just as well as those with two.

Finally, DeMarco and Lister (1999, pp. 44–50) spotted something: there was something about the company itself that affected the coders' work. They went digging for more, and here's what they found:

- When asked whether they had a quiet workspace, 57% of the most successful coders answered yes. And the least successful coders? 29% of them had a quiet space to work.

- When asked if they had a private workspace – possessing the ability to block out the distraction that comes with interruption – 62% of the most successful coders answered yes. The figure for the least successful coders was 19%.

- And when asked if they could divert or ignore their phone calls, 76% of the most successful coders said they could. Only 19% of the least successful were able to do this.

The results are clear. Better work was being produced not because of salary or experience, but because of environment. Well-designed solo workspaces mean better outcomes.

PASSPORT STAMP – TAKING CARE OF YOUR HEALTH

Intention – look after yourself by knowing how the system works *before* you get ill or have an injury. All of the below is important, not an optional read.

Action – first, remember that physical health is the basis of everything: without this, you won't have good mental health or be able to learn or have general good times. So, eat a good diet and get enough sleep. Get enough fresh air and sunlight for your vitamin D. We know you know this already, but some students seem to forget it entirely as soon as they set foot on campus.

Sign up to a GP surgery, which might be at the university medical centre. Learn how their appointments system works, as there is no standard method. You might need to phone, fill in a form or show up in person to get an appointment. Find out how long you typically have to wait for an appointment, and what to do if the situation is too urgent to wait. Know where your nearest accident and emergency (A&E) unit is, and how you would get there. Be clear in your own mind what kind of medical problems require what kind of attention:

- Emergency – if life-threatening, including heavy bleeding – call 999.

- Urgent healthcare advice for something non-life-threatening – call 111.

- Urgent injury – go to A&E.

- Non-urgent problem – NHS walk-in centre (there aren't many of these, but search Google Maps to find your nearest one) or GP surgery.

- Mental health problem – speak to your GP and the university counselling service.

- Specific needs – there will be specialist and confidential sexual health clinics (including STD screening, emergency and non-emergency contraception), physiotherapists, psychiatrists, travel inoculation clinics and so on accessible through the university medical centre.[1]

Set up your online medical services through the NHS app so that any prescriptions go automatically to a nearby pharmacy, where you can pick them up after a day or two. You can order repeat medications online, if they have been pre-approved by the GP.

Students who are going away from home for the first time, and who are under 25, are eligible for a vaccine to prevent meningitis. It could save your life. It is also recommended that you check whether you have previously had two doses of the MMR vaccine, and that you have an annual flu vaccine if you have various health conditions. If you are under 25 and have not had the HPV vaccine, you might want to do that too. And while we're on the subject of contagious diseases, we assume that we don't need to give you the condom talk.

You should also sign up to a dentist, but in some parts of the UK it will be hard to find an NHS practice that is taking on new patients. If you can't get a dentist and have a dental emergency, try calling 111 for advice, or in some areas there may be a local dental helpline you can try.

Reflection – do you know what you would do if you had a very high fever, or a sports injury, or an unexpected rash? You need to know. Are you living in a way that respects and protects your own health and wellbeing? Don't take good health for granted. OK, lecture over!

---

1   See https://www.nhs.uk/nhs-services/getting-medical-care-as-a-student/.

THE ATTENTION ECONOMY AND YOUR DIGITAL ENVIRONMENT – HOW TO BEAT DISTRACTION

Back in Victorian Britain, children were exploited by the super-rich – made to toil in mills and factories, completing monotonous tasks. The pay was so poor, their bosses became incredibly wealthy. Fast-forward two hundred years and instead of overseeing work in mills, social media companies encourage vast numbers to work for them for free: making videos, taking pictures, watching content and improving advertising algorithms.

This is no longer a manufacturing economy; it's an attention economy.

The more you scroll, the more money social media companies can charge for advertising, and the more their chief executives and share-holders make. Putting in a hard day's work in the salt mines of social media can leave you drained, dispirited and down ... while thousands of miles away in Silicon Valley your boss sips a piña colada by the swimming pool.

If you've accidentally become a committed employee of one of these billionaires, it could be your digital environment that's intruding upon your study. You might have the calmest, most private and inspiring study spot on the whole of campus, but if you take your phone along and find yourself manipulated into working wage-free for someone else, you're not going to have the time or concentration to do the work that improves your own life chances.

Travelling while looking at your phone isn't really travelling.

TASK

AUDIT YOUR DIGITAL ENVIRONMENT

Place your phone and your notebook and pen in front of you. Like a digital detective, you're going to examine the phone as if it doesn't belong to you. What does this device tell me about its owner?

Under 'settings' you'll be able to find information about screen use and digital wellbeing, which tells you exactly how much time this person spends on their phone and, more importantly, which apps they use the most. Explore this and make notes.

Critically assess the screen layout. Phone users tend to put the apps that consume most of their time front and centre. Ask yourself questions like:

- What apps appear immediately on the first screen?
- Which are the one-touch apps, permanently displayed for easy access?
- Which apps has this person put into folders, requiring an extra touch to reach?
- Which are on screen two, requiring a swipe to get to?
- Which are on screen three?
- What is the opening screen designed to lead the phone-user to do?

Continue to note your findings. As you do, you might begin to see the device with fresh eyes, which means you can begin a redesign.

Consider the following:

- Promoting apps linked to study, reading or exercise to the first screen. Moving others further back.
- Redesigning folders so that certain apps are harder to access. Move these folders to screen two or three, so a swipe is needed too.
- Reducing the number of apps on the first screen. Changing your screen settings to black and white.
- Changing screensavers and background images to emphasise the change you want to make – a picture that reminds you of the destination you want to reach, or an inspiring quote (so, not 'live, laugh, love').

◼ Deleting apps and only using them on your laptop. Perhaps having a time of day you check in with them, for twenty minutes only.

AEROPLANE SETTINGS AND OTHER BLOCKERS

Once, we were trying to track down a particular student. Over the last term, he'd transformed himself into an excellent scholar, producing really impressive work with each submission. We needed to ask him for help on a particular project and knew he was somewhere on campus. We ran into one of his friends and asked where he was. She texted him and, getting no reply, rolled her eyes. 'Aeroplane settings again,' she said.

It turned out that this was part of the reason why he'd become so successful. He'd started small – aeroplane settings for fifty minutes after lectures. Now he was on aeroplane settings for three hours daily between lunch and 4 pm. None of his friends knew exactly where he worked, but they all knew about his new approach to concentration, and that he'd reappear soon enough.

There are apps that can help you to do this too: Forest is one we've seen work well, but there are plenty of others. If you've got a problem with your digital environment, this approach could work for you too.

Begin by using aeroplane settings three times a week. Screen-free travel makes the best memories.

PASSPORT STAMP – JOIN IN A NEW CULTURAL ACTIVITY

Intention – develop a new interest, feel con-
nected and form a network of like-minded people who also want to
learn about whatever it is – Africa Society, Biohacking Society, Ceilidh
Band, Doctor Who Society (all real Oxford University societies) and
so on.

Action – most universities have societies running into the hundreds.
Make a shortlist of cultural activities that you think you might find
interesting but haven't had any involvement with yet. This could
cover a huge range of things: at your university there'll be players of
Dungeons & Dragons and other board game enthusiasts, there'll be
film clubs, scuba divers, paintballers and faith groups. You might
want to join a band or chat with music enthusiasts, poets and novelists. Aspiring journalists will be running university magazines and
newspapers, there'll be political groups, eco-activists, artists and
designers. Fashion students will need models, bands will need sing-
ers and musicians, the university TV channel will need presenters
and writers, the radio station will need DJs, and the Harry Potter
Society will have a shortage of people who identify as Slytherin.

Don't feel the need to be too earnest. If the Marxism Club is the one
for you, fair enough, but be honest with yourself. If it's really all about
the Knitting Society, just go for it – this activity should be about relax-
ation, joy, escapism and connection. Start by going to one session
held by one society, just to see. And then try a few more because not
all will be well-run or happening regularly. Some will almost certainly be flaky, boring or snobby, but at least you gave it a go and now
you can move on.

Reflection – were your experiences interesting? Did they make you
happy? Could a particular society sustain your interest for a little
while? Did you feel like you had found your people? These aren't
make or break decisions, but could lead to who knows what unfore-
seen joys, so just get stuck in. People often find lifelong friends or
partners in these settings.

ACTIVITY 1.10
ALL HANDS ON DECK
– FORM A STUDY GROUP

LEARN WITH OTHERS AND BOOST YOUR UNDERSTANDING

If you created an itinerary on page 41, or perhaps just imagined your pathway through your university course, reflect on whether you included other people and what parts they played. Did you see yourself travelling alone, perhaps on a solo voyage without the aid of a navigator? Were other people around, but delaying your progress?

Although you bear the most responsibility for your own direction of travel, the reality is that you will be surrounded by people who could help you if you seek them out and take some proactive steps. It helps if you see the benefits of cooperation over competition.

In Sam Conniff Allende's brilliant book about teamwork, *Be More Pirate*, he writes about how the pirate code allowed shipmates to organise, mobilise and draw strength from the group without sacrificing individuality:

. . . .

The pirates knew what was expected of them ... they used their codes to ensure their missions were a success and they made sure to update and adapt them to prevent them from becoming redundant, limiting or outdated ... (Conniff Allende, 2018, p. 227)

. . . .

So during the golden age of piracy, groups of highly rebellious individuals charted successful courses over the high seas, operating within an agreed set of rules.

Once you've begun to form a sense of who your fellow students are, think about which of them might make good study-buddies. It's time to muster your crew.

BUT I LIKE TO TRAVEL ALONE!

You might have operated that way up until now, but you should be more open-minded about how you can improve your own skills as a group member or leader. On some undergrad courses, you might find that group work is promoted or even required for some assessed work (see Levin, 2004). It is no doubt true that many employers will be keen to see evidence of teamworking.

What you need here is a healthy combination of humility and self-confidence. You should feel that you have something valuable to offer, while acknowledging that you have a great deal to learn from your peers' ideas, habits and insights. Believe us, both of these statements will undoubtedly be true. You can help others understand difficult topics and, in doing so, expand and deepen your own understanding.

In addition, having a self-timetabled study group is motivating because you will have to set yourself regular deadlines to prepare work for the group meeting. If you do it right, a study group can be supportive, confidence-building and even enjoyable.

TASK

Decide on a broad **aim** for the group and write it down in one sentence. It doesn't need to be detailed, and you might want to refine it in your first meeting. The initial purpose is just to be clear in your own mind so that you can explain your plan to potential recruits and start everyone off on the same footing. Here's an example:

> To discuss points raised during the previous week of lectures, so that we can share our ideas and resources, work through problems and expand our notes.

In other words, the aim needs to set out an intention to form a happy band of fellow travellers working towards the same goal.

Approach no more than four **recruits** and ask them to join. This might feel challenging, but what's the worst they can say – 'No, thanks.'?

Remember, you're looking for fellow backpackers, not tourists; people who could bring qualities like creativity, positivity, kindness, intellect or leadership. Those with good cooperation skills may be better study-buddies than the academic 'stars' of the course. They need to be personable and responsible ... it's not comfortable to go on a long voyage with crew who are flaky, disorganised or overly commanding.

You might end up asking more people if some of the first lot turn you down. Don't take it personally. If they're not interested, they weren't going to be right anyway. If they say yes, add them to a WhatsApp group, or similar, and fix the time and place of the first meeting ASAP, before they change their minds or go off on somebody else's ship. Aim to end up with three to five people in total.

Arrange to **meet** somewhere suitable – this is a work thing! For the first meeting, you should take the lead, but it might be that another leader emerges in future, or that you take it in turns to steer each session. You might not always be at the helm, but for this first meeting it's all on you, so think about structuring it so everyone can speak. Here is your agenda:

- Discuss the group's **ongoing aims** and write them down.

- Decide on the ground rules or a **charter** for the group – for example, how you will communicate, how often you will meet, that you will all attend or give apologies for absence, and so on. Assign specific roles so that everyone knows who will be doing what. The charter of pirate Bartholomew Roberts from February 1722 included a variety of items, from 'every man has a vote in affairs of moment' to 'no striking one another on board' (Conniff Allende, 2018, p. 219), so think along these lines! Try 'criticism should be constructive' and 'each member contributes to discussions and preparation work'.

- Decide on **topics** to cover next time and how this will work – for example, will you each take a different sub-topic to research and report back on? How will you share ideas, resources and findings? You should think about setting up an online Miro board or similar, which you can all access and edit (see our example on page 62).

Once you get going, you'll find that difficult course content or assignments will feel much lighter, because you are sharing the load and inspiring each other. However, do remember when sharing notes that you must be scrupulous to avoid plagiarism. Your university will have clear guidelines about this, and they won't mess about – it's a serious matter.

Finally, don't be discouraged if someone drops out; just recruit a new member as soon as you can.

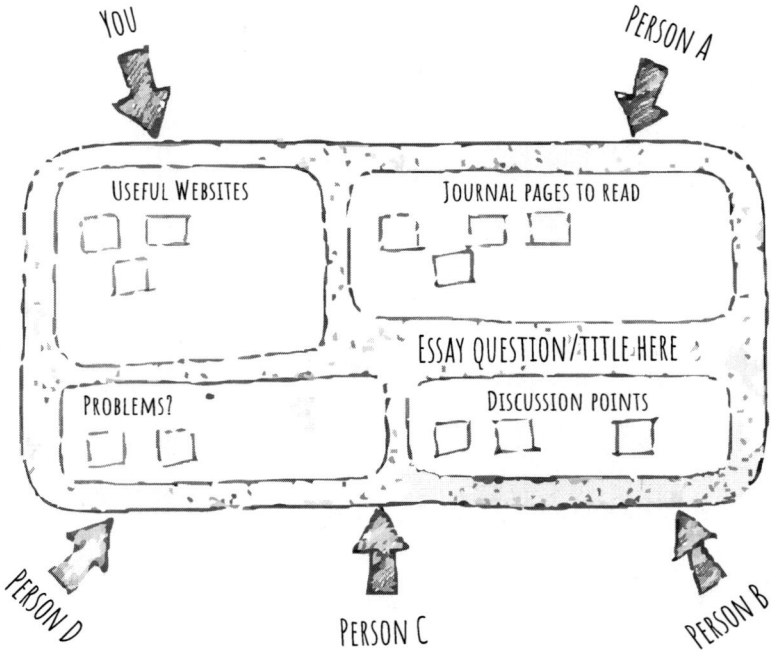

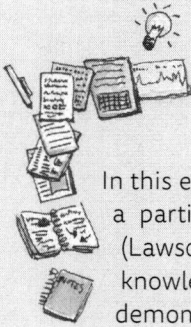

RESEARCH CORNER – KNOW IT WELL ENOUGH TO EXPLAIN IT OUT LOUD

In this experiment, participants were asked to explain how a particular everyday object – a bicycle – functioned (Lawson, 2006). Everyone who took part had to rate their knowledge of pedal bikes on a scale, then attempt to demonstrate their understanding by simply drawing one.

That's it. All they had to do was draw a bike, but the results were fascinating. There was a huge proportion of errors. People with a high level of confidence in their knowledge of how bikes work still produced inaccurate drawings, with pedals in the wrong place, the chain connecting the front and back wheels, a misunderstanding about how brakes work or an illogically shaped frame. This despite the fact that bikes are visually distinctive, and that many of us own one, can ride one, or at least see them every day.

If you try it yourself, you'll see. We often think we understand how something works up until the point at which we have to demonstrate that knowledge or understanding to others. The researcher goes on to cite a similar study (Marmie and Healy, 2004) in which participants had to remember what coins had engraved on their surfaces. They 'found that recall of the features of coins and their spatial position was much improved after just 15 sec[onds] of intentional learning and that intentional study produced large benefits, even when recall was delayed by one week.' (Lawson, 2006, p. 1673)

So we might think we know something, but it's only in demonstrating that knowledge by explaining it to others that we realise we need to study it again.

That's why study groups work. Their participants spend a lot of time doing *intentional* study, explaining parts of the course to one another, verbally going over what's been taught, correcting one another's errors and strengthening their collective knowledge.

PASSPORT STAMP – LOCAL CUISINE

Intention – experience the delights of local food traditions without getting food poisoning or busting the budget.

Action – if you are at a city university, there will likely be a cluster of multicultural food options aimed at students and very close at hand. Sometimes whole streets of it. We recall with fondness Cardiff's Chip Alley and Manchester's Curry Mile. The beauty of studying in any UK city is that almost the whole world is right there, through opportunities to eat food from all corners of the globe, albeit of massively varying quality and authenticity. The basic rule here is to try new things but stick to your budget for each meal. Consider how often, realistically, you can afford to do this, by doing the actual numbers and writing them down somewhere you can refer back to. Look out for student offers and take advantage of vouchers and early evening prices, if they apply. Bad stomach the next day? Don't go back!

Reflection – eating together can be a lovely way to bond with new friends, so do treat yourself to meals out if you enjoy it. It's very easy, though, to splurge on eating out and takeaways rather than cooking for yourself, so use your cash wisely and keep track of your spending. Be honest, how much of this is justified? Don't be lured into overspending in an effort to keep up with your apparently wealthy new friends. It won't end well. See also Passport Stamp – Home Cooking, on page 103.

ACTIVITY 1.11

SCHEDULING YOUR WEEK – HOW TO GET THE MOST OUT OF YOUR TIME

In your travels up to this point, almost all of your scheduling has been done for you.

Remember those carefree days when school took thirty hours of your time each week and told you exactly where to be and what to do? All 100% of your study time sorted – from 9 am until 3 pm. You got no say, but you also had no responsibility.

Once you reached seventeen or eighteen, you might have had, say, twenty-four of your thirty hours scheduled for you, and you had six hours of free periods to manage yourself. You probably messed up to begin with, using them all as 'frees' before figuring out you'd have to do *some* work and then finally getting to grips with it.

If you've been in the workplace, you will probably have found that some-body else controlled your day-to-day schedule too.

Things are likely to be very different now.

Depending upon your university and course, you might have, say, twelve of the thirty hours scheduled. In other words, you'll be doing the majority of your timetabling yourself. Tourists struggle with this. They hang about waiting for further instructions or for someone to give them some atten-tion. One problem with this approach is that by 2029 university is projected to cost about £10,500 in fees each year in the UK, and a 'year' is equivalent to roughly 150 days of teaching.[1] That's £70 a day. Waiting around doing nothing is expensive.

---

1   See https://www.theguardian.com/education/2024/nov/04/university-fees-in-england-to-rise-next-autumn-for-first-time-in-eight-years.

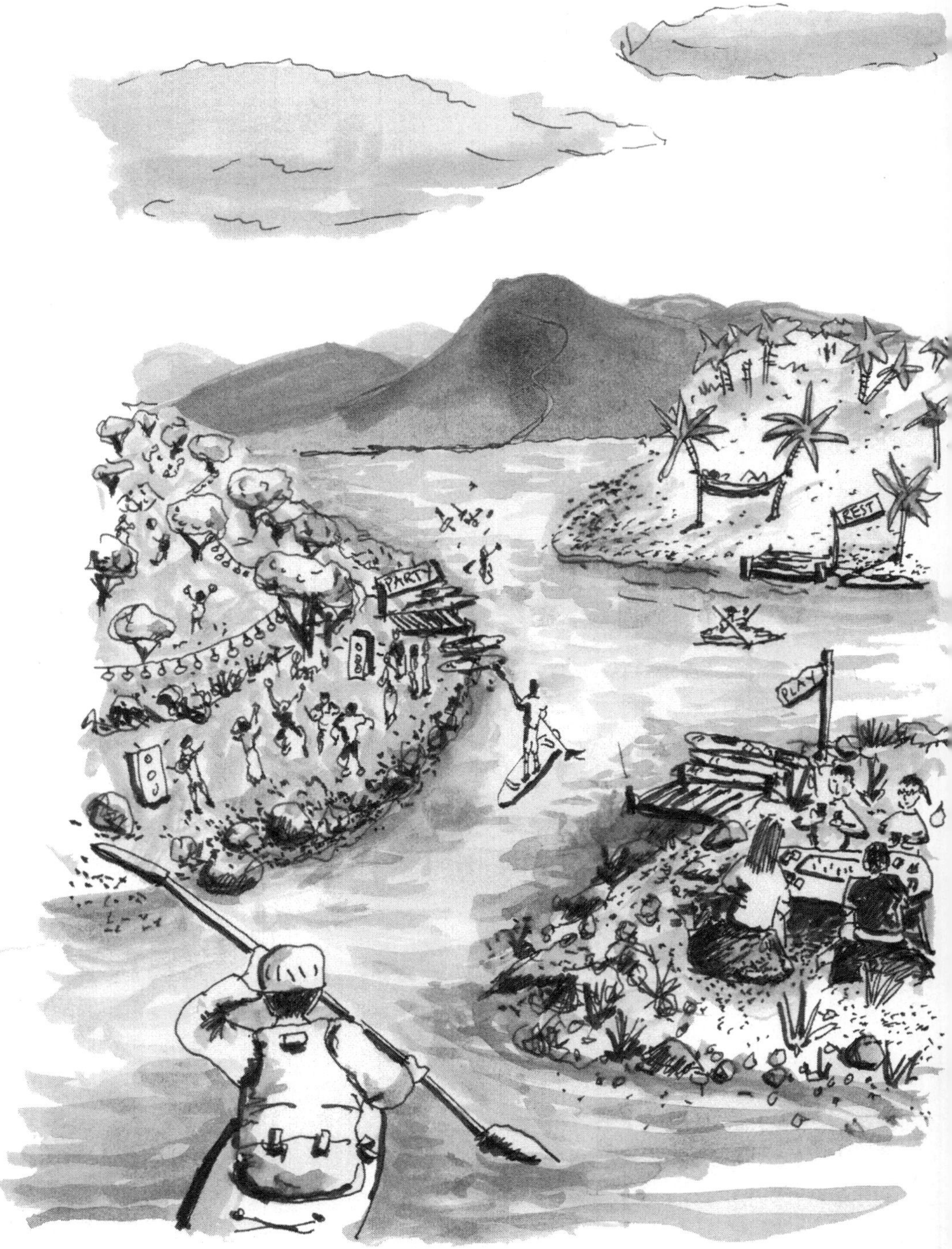
PARTY
REST
PLAY

TASK

You'll need to schedule your non-contact time to get the most out of your university experience. You might not like the sound of some of the ideas below – no worries. Pick and choose the ones that are going to work for you:

After every lecture, schedule half an hour's thinking time. Grab a coffee, look over your notes and double-check that you understood it all before you get on with your day.

Schedule an hour at the end of each day to go over everything. A pocket of time for thinking about the day's key concepts and ideas, and clarifying your notes.

Schedule a meeting with a study group once a week. Make it just before lunch so you can get a bite to eat afterwards.

Schedule a daily VLE check. You'll be able to seek out answers to issues like: what exactly was the brief for this project? What deadline did that lecturer mention? What was the name of that documentary they recommended?

Schedule a couple of hours' hard work followed by a trip to the gym or cinema. Reward yourself for your efforts and make time for activities that will benefit your mental health.

Schedule reading and research time in the library. Have a non-negotiable time slot when, no matter how on top of things you are, you choose a quiet spot and spend ninety minutes reading.

Schedule a meeting with yourself. On the agenda: how are my studies progressing? What's going well? What can I do to improve matters?

Once you've considered all of these possibilities, choose a couple that you think will really work for you and make a commitment to them.

Once you're confident, you can begin navigating yourself towards interesting stop-overs on your study journey. Confident that you're on top of your work, you might schedule a stop-over that serves as a rest, a break to see friends or some other reward or celebration. Stop-overs like this can be truly enjoyed if you know your scheduling is strong.

THE POINTS OF YOUR COMPASS – WHO'S WAITING TO HELP?

Remember, you are supported as a learner *and* as a person by many different professionals and services at your university. It is not unusual for a new student to feel lonely or overwhelmed. Your personal tutor will make you aware of some of these services, but it can't hurt to think about how to find any specific types of support you might need.

The diagram on page 70 shows an example of a student at the centre of a supportive web of contacts who are there to help them with all kinds of problems: academic, personal and financial. It helps to make a compass diagram like this at the start of your course, because we all experience rough seas at times and it's good to have done the forward planning and be ready to deal with that.

TASK

DRAW A COMPASS FOR WHEN YOU ARE FEELING ALL AT SEA

Using the example on page 70 as a guide, draw the points of your personal compass. Place yourself at the centre and arrange around you all the people and services who you can go to for assistance or information. When we are floundering, we sometimes lack the clarity to find the right support or the impetus to ask for help. You could add the phone numbers, office locations or email addresses for each person, so that it's easy for you to make contact if you need to. All the people on the example compass are paid to help you – it is their job.

English language support centre
Personal tutor
Students' union advice centre
Subject librarian
YOU
Disability/dyslexia support service
University health centre or GP
University's student wellbeing service
Department welfare team

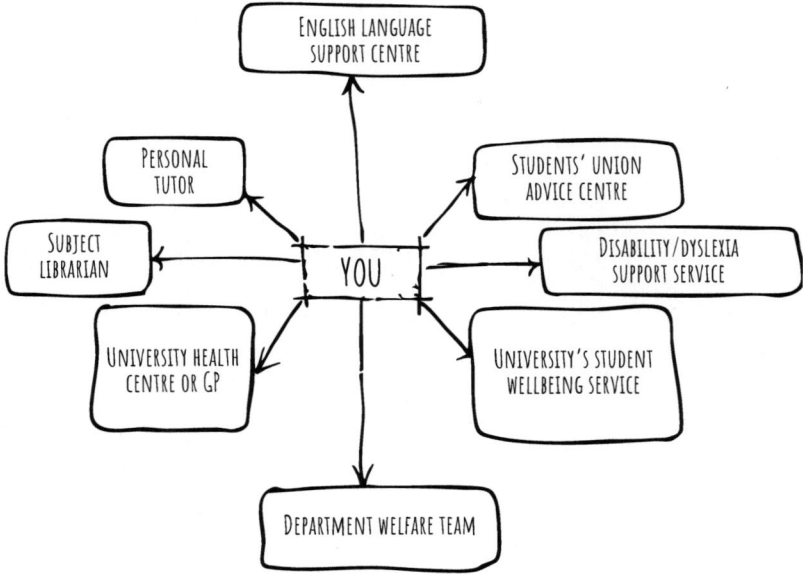

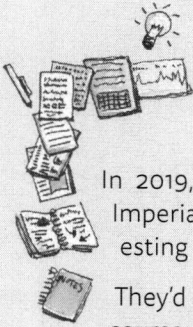

RESEARCH CORNER – THE IMPORTANCE OF ASKING FOR HELP

In 2019, academics from the University of Reading and Imperial College London published the results of an interesting study (Wong and Chiu, 2019).

They'd gathered together thirty students who were on course for the very best grades and interviewed each of them for ninety minutes. The students were asked about the same things: high school experiences, how university had been different, how they prepared for assessments, what feedback they'd been given, how they solved problems and, crucially, what advice they'd give to others.

These students were all on different courses – criminology, sociology, international relations, education – but their interview answers were surprisingly similar. What follows are extracts taken word-for-word from their advice to new students. The patterns are remarkable:

'They're lecturers, not mind readers ... talk to the staff in your modules, really speak up.'

'I've learnt to let other people look at my work ... [it] really helped.'

'If you need help, you need to go to the lecturer. They're not going to come find you if something is wrong with your essay ... you have to up your game now.'

'Don't be afraid to talk to your lecturers. You know, always communicate with your lecturers, tell them if you don't understand something.'

'Go and bother your lecturers and ask them to see drafts.'

We might often imagine that students who are on track to get the best grades are the ones who aren't asking for help – that they can do it without assistance. But this study, and others, shows that there tends to be a positive correlation between asking for help and achievement – and also a positive link between asking for help and feeling part of a supportive community, which in turn boosts feelings of optimism and belonging.

It may be a little frightening, but it'll be worth it. Ask for help!

PART TWO
OVER THE OCEAN

OK! You've started your journey – begun backpacking your way around campus, met new people and been to parties. Isn't it job done?

Not quite. Those first steps in a journey are important and exciting, and no doubt you've made a stellar start. But travelling can be hard. Often, it's the middle of a journey that gets you: it's missing the glitz and the glamour of the beginning, and it lacks the hope of triumph that comes towards the end. It's just ... the middle. It can feel a bit of a slog.

If you ever feel this way, reassure yourself. Your feelings are not unusual. In fact there's an old university cliché about the difficulty of the middle; you'll sometimes hear talk of the mid-term wobble.

So, in this section, we'll look at some of the skills and habits that will help you to get the most out of your studies as you make your way through the whole of your first year at uni. We will help you stay true to your plans for the full trip – middle and all – without straying too far off the beaten track.

In this part of the book, some of the sections offer advice to reflect on and others have a task attached. Read them all and return to them when you feel the middle of your journey is getting tough.

HOW TO READ

OK, so you thought you learnt this skill in your first year at school and have been using it ever since then. But higher education is likely to ask much more of your reading skills than ever before. Don't feel concerned by this. New learning situations always demand things from us that will make us feel uncomfortable to some extent – that's what learning is. Without reading, learning can be a superficial experience, lacking the depth and richness of understanding that you deserve to have.

So, how will things be different? Well, you could have a lot of different things to read in a short period of time. Some of these will be loooong pieces and you might want to tear your hair out while battling with them. This is normal. Then there's the fact that reading complex academic writing will likely be more of a challenge than you have experienced before – entire sentences won't make sense and you'll be looking up a lot of unfamiliar words. Don't stress, this is also normal. And a third thing. Back at school, you might have got used to doing a quick speed-read before moving on, but now you find yourself having to digest, interrogate, analyse and remember your reading matter because it forms the basis of assessed submissions. Again, normal.

So, difficulty with reading at this level is to be expected. But with a few adjustments to your approach, you'll soon acclimatise.

ASSESSING YOUR READING LIST

Think of a reading list as being a little like a travel guide. You know the type of thing: a *What to do in New York*, but for a topic rather than a place. Travel guides often split their recommendations into subgroups, like this:

- There are the must-see sites: the Empire State Building, the Statue of Liberty, Central Park, Times Square.

- Then there are make-time-for sites: the Brooklyn Bridge, Broadway, the Metropolitan Museum of Art.

- Then there are other attractions, the neighbourhood gems: Little Italy, Chinatown, the High Line.

Reading lists have their equivalents – the must-see texts that are non-negotiable reading, the make-time-for texts that play a supporting role and the neighbourhood gems that are a little bit more specialist. The trouble is that university teachers might not clarify which are which and no two lists will work the same way. This makes navigating them a little tricky, so consider this broad advice when assessing your reading lists:

- **Think before you dive in.** Don't attempt to just start at the top of the list and read everything on it in order. There could be some cases where a list has been deliberately sequenced to match up to teaching sessions, so you might have to read lots of shorter pieces each week. However, if a list looks impossibly long, it's probably because it *is*. If you had a week in New York, you couldn't see everything. It might be the same with your reading list, so …

- **Know your must-see texts.** Have a look for the reading that is identified as 'key' or 'core' and commit to doing it. If these phrases aren't used, look for books, chapters or journal articles that keep getting mentioned. The more times a text is referenced, the more must-see it is.

- **Figure out the make-time-for texts.** These are going to be well worth exploring, depending upon the focus of your assignments, so assess which ones might be the most useful. You'll get better at this with experience.

- **Assess the neighbourhood gems on your list.** These can be fascinating deep dives. But, equally, you might encounter some reading recommendations that are quite niche. We're trying to be polite, but if you suspect something was written by a long-departed professor, has been on that list since 1943 and is now out of print … give it a go if it's relevant to a particular interest of yours; otherwise, leave it for now.

- **Sequence your reading.** Try comparing the book titles on your reading list to upcoming lecture titles. This will help you to work out an appropriate order.

- **Schedule reading sessions.** That way, no matter what's going on in a day, or what mood you're in, you'll commit to an hour's reading or more. (If you haven't read the previous section on scheduling time, jump to **ACTIVITY 1.11** on page 65.)

- **Reserve texts.** If any of your readings come in paper copies only, make sure you reserve one ASAP – there will be a few in the library, but there'll be a scrum of students attempting to access them.

- **Buying new books is a last resort.** Previous adventurers often sell their old books, and your uni email address will give you access to a wealth of e-books and online material.

However much prioritisation you do, you will still be looking at lots of reading. Accept this fact. Here is a basic strategy to help you:

1 **Skim-read where it's reasonable to do so.** For example, academic journal articles and chapters in edited volumes usually offer short descriptions (abstracts) of the content at the start of the paper or in the introduction. Skim these to check the relevance before you get stuck in.

2 **If stuck, seek out summaries.** These could be digested versions of the book, online videos or lectures. Treat these as a way into the text, not as a substitute, and only use trusted sources. You could also make summaries with the help of your study group.

3 **Take notes as you read.** This is essential, otherwise you will lose track of where you got important ideas and information from, and you won't be able to reference them correctly, or even remember them at all. And then …

4 **Revisit, organise and consolidate those notes.** This will help you to recall, reflect on and synthesise the things you have read. This is where the real work lies when you are producing an essay or report, for example. For note-taking advice, read on.

After all of this, you are still likely to encounter some tricky reading. The content is supposed to stretch your capabilities. If you can't find a way into it, this is the kind of thing to raise within your study group or with a tutor. Write down, if possible, exactly what is difficult about that particular text, formulate that into questions and ask for help. Depending on how brave you are feeling, you could ask your questions via WhatsApp, email, discussion forum, study group meeting, or direct questions to the teacher in seminars and lectures.

It is *very likely indeed* that someone else will have been wrestling with the same thing.

PASSPORT STAMP – GET INVOLVED IN YOUR STUDENTS' UNION

Intention – meet good fun and well-connected people, give something back/pay it forward, pursue political, charitable or journalistic ambitions.

Action – first read up on what goes on in your union building and go to any events that are publicised. For many, the union is just a place to eat and drink, maybe dance, but (depending slightly on where you are studying) you could find a huge range of interesting stuff going on. Opportunities to be a part of it all will be promoted at the start of the academic year, so don't miss the chance to write for the student newspaper, volunteer in the community, be an academic rep, offer your skills as an adviser, raise funds for a good cause or get part-time work that will help make you feel that you have a place in all of this. Talk to the relevant people and find a niche where you might be a good fit. This might feel quite challenging at first, but we promise you there are great rewards if you keep at it.

Reflection – do you feel excited by participating? Does it make you want to go back again and again? Does it feel good to be useful to others, whether paid or voluntary? Studies show that feeling useful is very good for mental health. In an analysis undertaken at the University of Oxford, 27 different studies were synthesised, finding that acts of kindness had a positive impact on the wellbeing of the actor (Scott Curry et al., 2018). Could there be something at the union that offers you better or broader prospects than you get from your academic course alone? Could you be dipping your toe into something that might end up as a calling or a career? This really is a one-off opportunity – seize the day, backpackers!

HOW TO TAKE NOTES

You will need to make a log of all the learning experiences on your adventure, so you can recall and enjoy it all when you reach port and sit those final exams. And a big advantage of making good notes is that it saves you time and stress. Accurately record your experiences in the moment and you spare yourself hours of confusing revision later in your journey.

But how do you take notes and then revisit and consolidate them? Try this:

CORNELL NOTES

Developed at Cornell University, this note-taking technique is almost the same as regular notes, but with an additional column – a couple of inches wide – on the far left of the page. It looks so simple; students often wonder what the point is ('Why leave an empty column while I take notes in the remaining space?') but we urge you to consider this approach. You can find online videos teaching you about the system, direct from Cornell University itself – well worth checking out – but for now, let's look at the process in more detail here.

IN THE MOMENT

As the lecture begins, add your additional column (often students do this by folding over the page on the left-hand side, leaving a long empty space). Take notes in the remaining space. You don't have to record everything – a tough ask! – instead, listen carefully and gather the big ideas. These might not be obvious immediately, but often it's the professor's tone, where they pause, their body language, repetition of key words and, of course, their presentation slides or board work that will give you the important clues you need. Lecturers tend to move through material pretty quickly – but don't worry, you'll get used to the speed of travel.

AFTERWARDS

The game-changer with the Cornell system is what happens after the initial note-taking. You could do this immediately after the lecture, at the end of the day or a few days later – see **ACTIVITY 1.11** on page 65 for further advice. Whenever it is you choose to return to your notes, here's where the empty column comes in. You'll go back over the notes, remembering the lecturer delivering the information, and begin to fill your blank column with two crucial things:

1 **Elaborations.** Add information or elaborate on existing information. Clarify definitions, add extra examples, visual summaries or boxes and arrows to emphasise what you think are the big ideas. This is best done with the aid of additional material. You might have the lecturer's slides, plus a textbook or an item from your reading list, so you're making the notes better – adding information and depth rather than just summarising what's already there.

2 **Test questions.** Write questions that you should be able to answer if you've remembered the material correctly. It's like setting a test for your future self or your study group. Next time you review the notes, you'll have a few challenging problems to consider and solve – a great strategy for revision.

And that's it. A note-taking system that builds in space for further reflection and testing. Simple, but hugely effective!

RESEARCH CORNER – IF YOU ONLY DO ONE THING, DO THIS ...

Academics at New York State's University at Buffalo studied the effects of note-taking techniques on students' test scores (Evans and Shively, 2019). The students were taught new information in the same social studies class but were asked to take notes in different ways:

- Group one took no notes at all.
- Group two took notes in whatever way they usually did. (None of these students used the Cornell technique. We'll call this group 'standard notes'.)
- Group three took Cornell notes, typing them digitally. They completed the additional column as they went along, not later.
- Group four took handwritten Cornell notes, again completing the additional column as they went along rather than later.

Then the students all took the same comprehension test. The mean score was 7.2 out of 10. The lowest score was 2 and the highest was 10. The researchers looked at the average scores achieved by the four groups. Here's what they found:

Group	Average student score as %
Group one: took no notes	58.7%
Group two: took 'standard notes'	70.7%
Group three: Cornell notes, typed digitally	76.1%
Group four: Cornell notes, handwritten	78.7%

And that wasn't all. Just before taking the test, the groups were asked to fill out a questionnaire about how well-prepared they felt, scoring themselves on a 1–5 scale. Group four, the handwritten Cornell notes group, were already feeling good; 56% of students scored themselves a 4 or 5. In group three, another Cornell notes group, 50% scored themselves 4 or 5. Then the scores drop. Group two, the standard notes group, had 45% of its members feeling positive. Unsurprisingly in group one, who hadn't taken any notes, 13% scored themselves 4 or 5 (Evans and Shively, 2019, p. 18).

So Cornell notes leave you feeling more confident, as well as significantly impacting how much you can recall from a lecture. It requires no extra effort but encourages you to think differently – and every little helps.

ACTIVITY 2.3
AEROPLANE SETTINGS
- HOW TO BUILD CONCENTRATION

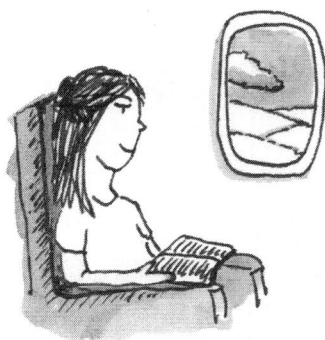

When it comes to developing your concentration, a good start might be to figure out your baseline, so you can measure your improvement.

Find a quiet place to study, with no sensory cues to disturb you. Select something you want to work on (reading, annotating, writing, whatever). Switch all phone alerts off and activate aeroplane settings. Start a timer, place the phone face down nearby and begin work. Next time you touch your phone, check how long you lasted. That's your starting point.

Don't despair if it's four minutes, or six, or ten. Concentration is like a muscle. It just needs a bit of training. The table on pages 84–85 provides a guide to how you might structure your workouts.

Stage and targets	Rough rules
Stage 1: twenty-five minutes on, five minutes off	Set a countdown for twenty-five minutes and put your phone on aeroplane settings. Allow yourself a time check now and again. But you have to go back to the start if: ▪ You stop working and abandon the session. ▪ You open any app on your phone. Consider blocker apps to help with this – Forest, for example.
Stage 2: fifty minutes on, ten minutes off	Set a countdown timer for fifty minutes and activate aeroplane settings. ▪ Allow yourself a couple of time checks but nothing else. ▪ Go back to the start if you cheat by opening any app. Feel free to go back to twenty-five-minute sessions if this stage feels too hard.
Stage 3: ninety minutes on, twenty minutes off	This time you're setting your countdown for ninety minutes ... or perhaps you've got to the stage where you feel you don't need one at all. Keep aeroplane settings on, but: ▪ Dealing with disturbances for a brief moment or two might be OK. ▪ However, do all you can to minimise them. Plan a reward at the end – maybe a bite to eat, a cup of coffee or a meeting with a friend?

	Things to consider
	Don't punish yourself if you fail and restart a few times – it's quite normal. Try diving into another twenty-five-minute session after a short break. Bear in mind that you might need longer breaks between sessions to begin with. Keep practising until you can do twenty-five minutes … it might take a week or two to get there!
	Consider choosing an off-the-beaten-track study location for your first few fifty-minute sessions. When you're starting out, give yourself an advantage by choosing work you're already engaged with and looking forward to exploring. Wear headphones when necessary to block out distractions, but don't depend on these.
	Location is important. Get picky about the quality of light, the feeling of calm silence, the space to spread out notes, the opportunities to stretch your legs, the view from the window. You're going to tire as the session goes on, particularly if you're working on something hard, so pack snacks for the journey – a bottle of water and something nutritious to keep you going is ideal.

Work slowly through the stages and you'll find your ability to concentrate gradually improves. It's like a workout for the mind – it will leave you tired but, hopefully, feeling positive and energised. And feeling on top of your work, which helps immensely with anxiety.

SCANNING AND PLANNING
– HOW TO STAY ON TOP OF WORK

The backpacker spends a lot of time curiously exploring the world around them – but they also take time to check the direction of travel, look ahead and scan the horizon. They refer to their map to assess their current position and plan their next steps.

You'll be learning a few different things at once and will have assignments involving different topics and deadlines. You'll often be jumping between them, and you won't be able to complete your work in one sitting. This means you'll often be starting something then coming back to it later. It's so easy to forget where you were up to, what you were doing and why you were doing it.

Scanning and planning helps you to record your progress, look ahead and figure out what to do next. This next task shows a simple way to do it.

TASK

RECORD KEEPING

You'll need to keep a record for *each and every task* you've been assigned (anything that will take more than one sitting to finish – a paper, a reading assignment, an extended essay, a design submission, whatever). You could use a notebook page, a productivity app or an online document.

Record three things: what the project is, where you're up to and what your next steps are, like so:

Project:
Here you add a description of exactly what the project is and what needs doing.

Details and deadline:
Here you record any crucial instructions you had – reminders your professors gave you, specific requirements or the project brief, word count requirements, etc.
Make a note of exactly when you need to submit.

So far:	Next steps:
Here you list the actions you've already taken – these work as a reminder of what you've done, so when you return to the project you quickly remember what progress you'd made.	*Here you record the one or two things you were planning on doing next the last time you worked on the project.*
	You'll return to the project, review your next steps and quickly know where your head was at.

Have one of these for every task you've got, and you'll never lose track of where you are.

STAGING YOUR DEADLINES

When it comes to submissions, remember to think in three delivery stages. If your deadline is a month away, break down your project into three parts and give yourself a deadline for each.

You might want an end-of-week-one deadline, by which time you will have finished the research and reading; an end-of-week-three deadline, when you commit to having a rough and ready draft complete, then the real deadline might be a week later.

You're much less likely to miss the real deadline if you think in three delivery stages and hit your self-imposed deadlines.

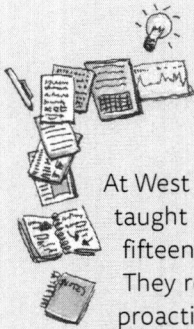

RESEARCH CORNER – THE POWER OF SCANNING AND PLANNING

At West Texas University, 210 undergraduate students were taught about scanning and planning in a series of three fifteen-minute sessions (Humpherys and Lazrig, 2020). They received some important study advice: about being proactive rather than waiting for help, about setting high standards and about planning delivery stages and taking first steps.

Each week, each student had to list all the projects they were working on, record the deadlines for these projects and then pre-plan some study time that week, figuring out where they were up to and what they needed to do next – basically, a system very similar to the one we've suggested in the task. Of course, as with all good pieces of research, there was a second group who weren't given this guidance and were left to continue on as normal (the control group).

At the end of the semester, the researchers compared the two groups, measuring three things. First, they studied the percentage of missing assignments – the number of students who'd missed deadlines during that semester. Second, they looked at satisfaction – how students were feeling about their studies – and third, at their final grade.

The results were powerful. Scanning and planning halved the rate of missing assignments – a significant improvement. Furthermore, those students who'd been taught the additional sessions felt overwhelmingly more optimistic about their studies and recognised the impact that more effective time-management had had – over 85% reckoned that it had been positive. Finally, the students even received slightly higher grades – a 3% increase on their peers (Humpherys and Lazrig, 2020, pp. 48–49).

Fewer missed deadlines, a slight increase in test scores and a significant feeling of positivity? Results like those make scanning and planning well worth it.

GUIDE OR JUDGE? HOW YOU SEE YOUR PROFESSOR IS IMPORTANT

Academics can sometimes seem unapproachable because of things like the mysterious letters after their names, the many books they have published or maybe even their worldwide fame in their particular field.

It might feel daunting that your work will be assessed by this remote figure who commands respect/gets interviewed in the media/has a big corner office with loads of bookshelves. We remember a senior prof who had so many stacks of books and journals in his office that you could barely get in the door – they towered above the visitor in a fairly threatening way. Turns out, though, that the man himself was good-humoured and helpful.

So, it's time to get over yourself and drop this feeling of being daunted.

When your teacher sets you a piece of work, remember that they are your guide, not just the judge of the finished product. We come across this problem when we offer tutorials to help students with drafting their assessed work; some just don't turn up because they fear their half-complete work being judged in a negative way. These students need to realise that they are being offered guidance, not criticism.

Yes, it is true that the teacher sets the challenge and assesses the outcome, but in between, for perhaps 80% of the time, they are there as your guide. Maybe you are on a course that offers tutorial support as part of the teaching programme. If so, turn up to every opportunity to seek guidance. If not, you should still see that teacher as your guide, and approach them in person or by email to ask for help. For advice on how to ask questions, see **ACTIVITY 2.6** on page 93.

We have absolutely no doubt in our minds, from years of experience, that the students who ask the most questions end up being the most successful but also get the most enjoyment from their course. And that is the way of the backpacker.

TASK

Since they're there to guide, make appointments to see your lecturers.

Remember office hours from the phrasebook? Many of your teachers will have these arrangements set up. They will have blocked out and advertised periods of time when they're available to chat. You might find their office hours online or, if they're old-school, pinned up on their office door, with slots for you to put your name in.

Your peers will be doing this – and coming away with suggestions for how to improve, things to read or resources to check out. It's a mistake to think that 'being independent' and 'not asking for help' are the same thing.

Often the solution to a problem you have lies in an office hours appointment. That confusing brief that you can't get your head around? The mystery of why others seem to be getting better grades than you? The written feedback you don't understand? An office hours appointment could clear up any confusion.

OFFICE HOURS - A FIVE-STEP PROCESS

1   Find out when your teacher's office hours are.

2   Book a slot.

3   Transfer it to your calendar.

4   Set an alarm or reminder so you don't miss it.

5   Take notes during the session and reap the benefits!

ACTIVITY 2.6

THE INQUISITIVE BACKPACKER – HOW TO ASK QUESTIONS OF ACADEMICS

You've probably come across comedic depictions of the tourist who isn't willing to ask for directions – the traveller who is lost but won't ask for help.

But a backpacker really does need to be willing to seek help, whether they are in trouble or not. It might be that there is some wonderful attraction nearby that they don't know about, which they could go and see, and learn from, if only they asked. A tourist on their all-inclusive package holiday with pre-booked tours won't need to do this, but they are missing out on some great stuff! While they sit by the pool all day, you need to be out and about, seeking knowledge.

It might sometimes feel that other people have the knack of asking good questions, while you do not. You might feel pressure to sound intellectual and improve your standing in the eyes of others. Don't do this. Instead, go for directness and simplicity. If you aren't sure what we mean, on page 94 you'll find some micro-scripts that give you the dos and don'ts of how to ask. They are intended to steer you away from the unhelpful 'I just don't get this' state of mind to proactively request assistance.

Backpackers ask ...	Tourists think to themselves ...
'What kind of work will get the best marks for this submission?'	I wonder what's the minimum amount of work I can get away with doing.
'What search terms could I use to find the most useful information on this topic?'	Perhaps there's just one key book on the reading list. I hope it's entertaining.
'I find it hard to understand this part of the lecture/topic/ module. Please could you explain it again?'	I'm confused, but if I wait long enough, the feeling will go away. Somebody bring me a cocktail.
'Please could you rephrase that for me? I'm not getting it yet.'	I don't understand the task, but if I ask, I will look stupid. I'll keep my shades on and hope someone else says something.
'Please could you give some examples to help me understand that part of the lecture?'	I have no idea what this lecturer is talking about. It's probably their fault.
'Could you recommend an introductory reading on this topic, please?'	I still have no idea what this lecturer is talking about, and it seems like nobody else does either. I'll skip next week.
'How can I do further research on this one, please?'	I'm great at this. I'll show everyone how much I already know by raising my hand and giving my own views for a few minutes.

EXPECT CHALLENGING ANSWERS

Academics aren't going to pass up a golden opportunity to teach – and a student asking a question is one of those occasions. So don't be alarmed if your question is answered with another question. It's likely to be something that challenges your thinking, like this:

Student: Do you think I should include a reference to this study or not?

Professor: Interesting question. What do *you* think?

Or this:

Student: Should I begin by tackling this topic, do you think?

Professor: Hmm. What do you see as the advantages of doing it that way?

Or this:

Student: I've done the reading you recommended, but I'm really confused about this topic.

Professor: OK, could you identify exactly where the confusion arises?

You might feel frustrated at first. ('Why won't someone just tell me what to do?!') But each time the frustration grows, remember that your teachers are stretching your thinking, pushing you to consider a problem differently and encouraging independent thought.

Here's another example to consider.

You might not have heard of writer and movie producer Brian Grazer, but you'll probably know his work. He wrote or produced such movies as *Splash, 8 Mile, American Gangster, The Da Vinci Code, Apollo 13, Inside Man*...

the list goes on. Interviewed for YouTube channel Big Think, Grazer tells an interesting story about his university years.[1]

Grazer studied psychology at the University of Southern California (USC), and he was a real backpacker – constantly curious. There was a particular professor he found fascinating and wanted to learn more from. But he felt anonymous, just one of 300 students on his huge course. So he waited to approach this professor after he finished a class: 'And I say: "I'd really like to just have ten minutes – a coffee with you,"' Grazer tells Big Think. 'And I turned that ten minutes, I expanded it into about an hour-and-a-half conversation, which had greater value for sure than the year I spent in that classroom.'

Grazer's curiosity made him engaging and interesting to talk to. He ended up learning much more than his fellow students, expanding his understanding in a way they didn't.

You can try this too.

---

1   See https://www.youtube.com/watch?v=EPdNs93yyMw.

SCARED TO PUT A FOOT WRONG? WHY PERFECTIONISM IS ALWAYS UNHELPFUL

Becoming skilled and increasing knowledge can be a painful process.

This is because learning is iterative, meaning that you need to continually revisit challenges, each time accepting that you didn't complete them perfectly before and facing up to your own lack of skill or knowledge.

Nobody enjoys feeling ignorant or vulnerable, especially if they are used to easy success. But you will never reach a point where you have nothing more to improve. That just isn't a thing. You are always in a state of relative ignorance. It can feel like you are doing nothing but making a chain of never-ending errors – hence the pain.

If you have any perfectionist tendencies, this pain is even tougher. We suggest that in the context of learning there are three broad types of perfectionism. Read these through carefully and honestly assess whether they describe you. It's nothing to be ashamed of, or down about. It's normal human psychology to experience these feelings.

TYPE ONE SUFFERS FROM ASSESSMENT FEAR

This type of perfectionist assumes that each grade they get during the course is as important as their final result. They give too much importance to one 'bad' grade and may not take into account that assessments have different weightings. In the first year, it's often the case that your grades don't contribute to the final degree classification (although check your course handbook to confirm!). They've forgotten that after graduation, the only grade that will matter will be that degree classification. They do everything they can to make sure every single submission is as perfect as it can be:

■ They spend hours ironing out every little error.

■ They polish the work until it gleams, agonising over tiny changes.

- They avoid submission entirely if it looks like they aren't going to get a first.
- They criticise themselves for every dropped mark.

Type one perfectionists cheat their future selves by shutting off the learning that comes from making errors. The short-term gain – 'I submitted a perfect piece of work and will win the admiration of my teacher.' – is offset ten times over by the long-term loss: 'Mistakes are information and I have far fewer than everyone else to learn from.'

By the time you graduate, no one can remember what grades you got in the first year, including the teachers who marked the work. Everyone's moved on. It's forgotten.

TYPE TWO SUFFERS FROM STATUS FEAR

This type of perfectionist is concerned with their performance relative to others'. During school or college they got used to being the best, or close to the best, in class. But cohorts of university students have all done broadly as well as each other, so best in class might now seem average. This can be a painful change, and students who experience it often adopt adverse coping mechanisms:

- They subconsciously create circumstances which explain their underperformance. 'I didn't start the essay until last night and rushed it. Of course it's rubbish.'
- They direct criticism towards others. The lecturer took time off ill, the slides wouldn't download properly, the textbook was missing from the library, the seminar was poorly delivered ...
- They resent those students doing better than them, explaining away their success as luck or privilege.

It's so much better to simply accept your current circumstances. Learning isn't a competition but a process of cooperation. Your teachers will give you feedback that you can reflect on, and this will help you improve. The peers you're trying to beat may be able to teach you something. Read **ACTIVITY 1.10** on page 59 and consider setting up, or joining, a study group.

TYPE THREE SUFFERS FROM DECISION FEAR

These folk see their course as being like a long trek up a mountain. There are plenty of rewards, such as excellent views, great company and regular snack breaks. There is the massive sense of achievement upon reaching the summit, and they know that they have that to look forward to.

But there are several different paths up to the top, some of which will be 'better' than others, and every rest break means looking back and judging themselves harshly for the decisions they took. They can see other routes that they could have taken – they could have avoided that boggy ground! They call themselves an idiot. There are lots more decisions ahead, but they don't want to make them for fear of getting it 'wrong'.

But, of course, there is no 'wrong' and 'right' path. This is all just part of the trek, and you didn't know about the shortcuts at the time, so there's no point punishing yourself or overthinking every decision on the path ahead. Instead, remember that with every step you are getting fitter, stronger and more skilled at negotiating the way.

TASK

Learning is based on a simple idea: that you lack something. That some-thing is the skills and knowledge of your course. If you didn't lack them, you wouldn't need the course. But here you are studying it!

Understanding this could be helpful in allowing yourself to drop the perfectionism.

TYPE ONE: ESTABLISH MINIMUM STANDARDS FOR ACTION

Psychologist Dr David Maloney has some great advice for beating perfectionism.

In one of his very helpful videos, the snappily titled, 'The Importance of Reaching a Point in Your Day When You Feel Finished', Maloney (2024) argues that for type one perfectionists, work never ends.

Everything we produce could always be slightly better, so our self-talk becomes critical and negative, a little like this:

'You're not done yet. There's still loads to do and it isn't perfect yet. Keep going. Do more, do more!'

As a result, he says, we can never relax. So his advice is this: we should negotiate with ourselves what he calls 'minimum standards for action'. This means asking ourselves: 'What's the least I could do today to feel like I've made some decent, solid progress on this?'

Be clear and firm with yourself when you answer: 'One hour in the afternoon, reviewing my submission and double-checking it's clear and logical.' This becomes your minimum standard for action. When it's done, you're done with that project for the day.

Negotiate some minimum standards for action.

TYPE TWO: CHOOSE MASTERY GOALS OVER PERFORMANCE GOALS

There are different ways of setting academic goals.

Performance goals are those which target a statistical outcome, a score or grade, often relative to others. Here are some examples from a recent study of undergraduates setting themselves goals for an upcoming exam (Katz-Vago and Benita, 2023):

- ▓ 'To achieve above-average or even excellent grades.'
- ▓ 'To get more than 90.'
- ▓ 'To get more than 80, so as not to lower my GPA.'
- ▓ 'To get a 100.'
- ▓ 'To pass the exam period with an average of 90+ without retaking.'

Mastery goals are different; they target personal behaviours, skills or competencies. Here are some undergraduates quoted from the same study, setting themselves mastery goals for the same upcoming exam:

- ▓ 'To summarize all the lectures that I did not understand well.'
- ▓ 'To be knowledgeable enough to help others.'
- ▓ 'To apply the material based on a deep understanding of it.'

- 'To understand the material and not just to study for the exam's sake.'

The study suggested that this second type of goal reduces students' stress levels, keeps them focused on the process more than the outcome, ensures motivation and commonly leads to better grades.

Try swapping your performance goals for mastery goals.

TYPE THREE: USE THE CORRIDOR PRINCIPLE

The corridor principle is a metaphor that requires you to imagine decisions and opportunities as doors lining either side of a long corridor in front of you.

Perfectionists have a right door/wrong door way of thinking. Only one of these many doors, stretching off into the distance, is the correct one to take and all the others represent a step in the wrong direction. The result: stressful inertia – hesitating at the top of the corridor, imagining what's at stake if they choose the wrong door.

The backpacker has a bias towards exploration. They don't think of the doors as right or wrong; they're all just options to explore. They may feel fear, but they begin moving down the corridor with a view to the long-term, making decisions and exploring rooms, with no high stakes.

The result is that new opportunities present themselves: new doors they couldn't see from the top of the corridor, new spaces, new chances they hadn't perceived when they were standing still.

The corridor principle tells us that indecision isn't a good place from which to assess potential choices, movement is. Movement presents opportunities we can't see when we're static.

Imagine yourself on the other side of the decision, choice made. You're moving forward. New opportunities are presenting themselves. You're free from stress, you've escaped inertia, you're liberated.

Now make the decision and move.

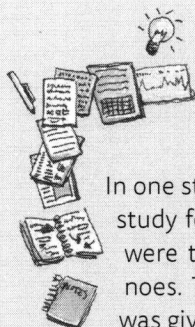

RESEARCH CORNER –
MISTAKES MAKE MEMORIES

In one study, 120 undergraduate students were gathered to study for a test (Wong and Lim, 2022). The material they were to be tested on was four paragraphs about volcanoes. They were split into three groups, and each group was given a different study technique.

- Group one had to read the text and rewrite it, underlining key phrases.
- Group two had to read the text and turn the material into a mind map.
- Group three had to read the text and take notes, making deliberate errors which they then had to correct. They had to record a crucial piece of information incorrectly (on purpose) then cross out the wrong version and write the correct information above it.

All three groups then had to write an essay on volcanoes, explaining the cause of an eruption. They got two scores: one for recall and one for application. Group three – the ones who made and corrected deliberate errors – got the top marks in both, by a long way. Why?

Mistakes, the researchers concluded, left distinctive memory traces because they forced students to process the information more rigorously, applying their knowledge. 'Considering what something *is not*,' they conclude, 'may enhance learning of the correct concept.' (Wong and Lim, 2022, p. 1827)

Making mistakes – and correcting them, of course! – while we take notes helps us to process information at a deeper level, therefore enabling us to learn it better.

Perfectionists expend vast amounts of energy avoiding errors ... and then miss out on the learning that those errors bring.

PASSPORT STAMP – HOME COOKING

Intention – stay healthy, have good energy levels and learn to host.

Action – if you haven't already learnt to cook a small range of cheap, healthy meals, you need to step up now. It's not hard. If you can successfully apply to uni, you can look up a recipe and follow step-by-step instructions. Here is how to get started.

Though you can find all the recipes you could ever need online, they can be annoying as they tend to require lots of scrolling through ads, and the ingredients are separated from the instructions by loads of 'blah blah blah' text. Then you end up with a phone covered in teriyaki sauce. Videos of methods present similar problems (although they could help if you are an absolute beginner). So get a cookbook – there are many good ones aimed at students and which cover all kinds of diets.

Plan ahead to buy ingredients, as those local mini branches of big supermarkets are often more expensive. If you shop in cheap places, you'll still find good quality food but your spend over a year will be way smaller. We recall a student who was known to only ever buy M&S food and was mocked mercilessly as a result.

Familiarise yourself with basic kitchen equipment. Don't be the person in the uni kitchen who sends a photo of a toaster to their dad, asking if it is a kettle (true story).

Once you have made a successful meal a few times over, think about inviting people around to eat with you. It's a kind thing to do and will cement friendships, even if your cooking is dead average. Just don't raise their expectations too high. We were once invited to 'dinner' by a student friend who had 'obtained' a catering-size stock of frozen breaded vegetarian fillets. They banged them in the oven and supplied them generously, with nothing on the side, not even cutlery. It was brilliant!

Reflection – can you make five different meals that cover all the basic food groups? Are there any green things in your repertoire? Is your food enjoyable? If not, you need to keep trying because not many people get rich enough to employ a personal chef. Is your cooking so bad that you are losing friends rather than gaining them? If so, maybe stop inviting people over for food and try another challenge instead.

ACTIVITY 2.8
THE LUCKY BACKPACKER – HOW TO BROADEN YOUR ATTENTIONAL SPOTLIGHT

Richard Wiseman, Professor of Psychology at the University of Hertfordshire, has spent a number of years researching luck. Does luck really exist, he wonders, or is it a psychological construct? His findings are published in *The Luck Factor: The Scientific Study of the Lucky Mind* (Wiseman, 2004).

Wiseman recruited four hundred people who described themselves in questionnaires as either exceptionally lucky or unlucky in life. His aim was to discover why these people considered themselves in this way.

After years of study, Wiseman concluded that lucky people aren't really lucky; they generate opportunities for positive things to happen, sometimes subconsciously, by noticing things around them. This ability to notice things, he concludes, is due to a person's attentional spotlight. All of us have an attentional spotlight. The world around us is so complex – full of sights, sounds and other sensory information – that our brain applies filters, simplifying what we see. Some people maintain broader attentional spotlights, seeing more of the world around them. Others have smaller attentional spotlights, perhaps due to feeling threatened or stressed, and they see less.

Here's an example of the attentional spotlight in action. Wiseman gave his subjects a newspaper and a simple task: count the number of photographs. What he didn't tell participants was that a few pages into the paper was a half-page notice, clearly printed in large letters. 'Stop counting,' it said. 'There are 43 photographs in this newspaper.' (Wiseman, 2004, p. 3)

Who saw this? The participants who considered themselves lucky. But they weren't luckier – they simply had broader attentional spotlights.

TASK

Wiseman found that people who considered themselves lucky spent time introducing variety and change into their lives. They explored new opportunities, tried different things or went to unfamiliar places. This meant their attentional spotlight was larger. Whereas repetition and familiarity will shrink your attentional spotlight, originality and novelty will broaden it.

The more interesting new opportunities you follow up, the 'luckier' you'll get.

What follows are five suggestions to broaden your attentional spotlight. Choose one idea and follow through. Really do it. Afterwards, reflect on the new things you've discovered, the new people you've met or the new opportunities you've stumbled across:

1   Walk into campus using a different route. Look for new shops, houses, cafes, museums or landscapes you haven't seen before.

2   Ask a friend from a different subject to give you a tour of their department. What are the fine art studios like? What are the fashion and textiles study spaces like? Ever wandered through the labs to see how the scientists live?

3   Ask to audit a class or attend a lecture outside of your subject. (Auditing means attending lectures or classes but not getting a grade.) Eccentric professors often put on interesting lectures ... and there might be nothing to stop you dropping in. One university we know had a chemistry professor who used to put on what students called a 'whizz-bang' show. He'd throw chemicals together at the front, making mini explosions, smoke and strange coloured flames. Loads of non-scientists used to go along just to witness the weirdness.

4   Attend a guest talk. Universities are likely to have a programme of visiting speakers – experts who turn up to share their insights. Famous writers, scientists, world leaders or political thinkers might be on your campus at some point. Show up and see what you can learn and who you can meet.

5   Visit campus at the weekend. It's so different. Walk through the canteens, corridors and workspaces with fresh eyes. You might spot posters you've always walked past, groups of postgraduates working on interesting projects, or screens advertising events you've never noticed.

PASSPORT STAMP – EXPLORE THE CITY

Intention – get to know where all the fun stuff is and, crucially, how to get there. Introduce your new friends and acquaintances to said fun stuff, persuading them to try it with you. In this way, get a reputation for being a good person to know, while having a ball.

Action – this is going to vary a lot depending on what you consider to be a pleasurable activity. We suggest being open minded about it. Maybe you already know that you love tenpin bowling and sculpture galleries, but you could also consider what night clubs and hat-making museums have to offer. So long as it's legal and affordable, there don't really need to be any rules. Allocate yourself an entertainment budget that allows you to do at least one fun thing every weekend. Save cash by taking your own food and walking or biking to places as much as you can. This also means you'll get to know the city quicker and notice all kinds of things to do that you might have otherwise missed. This will entail a fair bit of asking around (a good conversation starter) but also a little web-based research, so do put the time in. Googling 'free stuff to do in Manchester', for example, gave us twenty decent hits.

Reflection – just keep doing this all the time, occasionally pausing to check that it was indeed both legal and affordable. Was it? Carry on. Life is more than just work and we all need some fun.

ACTIVITY 2.9

THE BACKPACKER'S GUIDE TO REVISION, PART ONE

PIN BOARD
BOOKSHELF
GOOD LIGHTING
COMFY CHAIR
PLANTS NEARBY
FRESH AIR
READING CHAIR
PHONE ON AEROPLANE SETTINGS

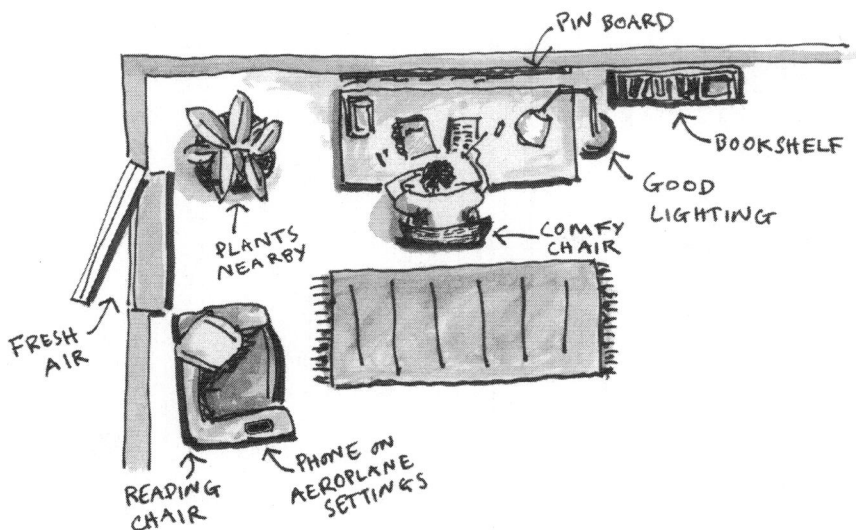

Aargh, not the R word! We do understand that this is nobody's favourite pastime, but if you are heading towards an exam or test, you already know that revision isn't something you can dodge. Most students are pretty terrible at it, thinking that as long as they've put the hours in, they've done the job. It isn't about the time spent, though; it's about the methods. So take the smart route.

First up, revision isn't one thing repeated, but a sequence of three phases. We cover them in the table on page 110.

Phase	Typical activities	% of revision time spent here:
One: rereading and refamiliarising	Reading class notes, underlining key ideas, highlighting important information, reading class textbooks or course guides, watching explanatory videos.	
Two: generating new material	Writing summaries of material, building your own study guide, writing information onto flash cards, turning information into tables, charts, posters, diagrams or mind maps.	
Three: testing recall, understanding and application	Covering up material and trying to recall it, setting yourself tests, talking through/teaching a topic out loud, working under timed conditions to solve problems, completing past papers or mock exam questions.	

Grab your notebook, think about your exam preparation so far and estimate what percentage of your study time you've typically spent in each phase. Scribble down some thoughts and a rough percentage for each stage.

Some students find themselves spending most of their time in phase one: a 70–30–0 split. When phase one dominates, you might find your attention dropping off as you read, or feeling so within your comfort zone that it's passive and boring.

Some students have done too much phase two revision in the past, reporting something like a 30–70–0 split. When phase two dominates, you might spend hours making flash cards that look beautiful or waste time copying them out again super-neatly, or redo mind maps or summaries over and over again.

If either of these sound like you, don't worry, that's normal. But remember, phase three will boost your learning most effectively. So if you feel yourself dawdling in phase one or two, push yourself to do some phase three work. Aim for a 30–30–40 split.

You won't necessarily want to! Setting yourself tests? Teaching a topic out loud? It sounds hard. You'll start coming up with reasons why you don't really need to. If this is you, it's normal to feel this way. Why? Because phase three revision strategies aren't comfortable or easy – they require effort.

But it's effort that will pay you back ten times over.

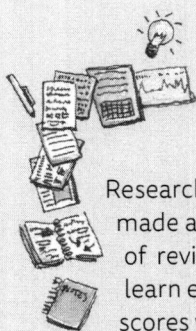

RESEARCH CORNER – PHASE THREE REVISION COUNTS

Researchers at the Ruhr University Bochum in Germany made a fascinating discovery about the three main phases of revision (Roelle et al., 2022). They had 158 students learn eight new concepts and then take a test. Their initial scores were pretty low as they'd only just encountered this material for the first time.

Then the revision began for a second test. The researchers were keen to see how different revision strategies boosted the original scores, so students were split into three groups. They each spent the same amount of time revising, but they did different things:

- Group one did phase one revision only. They read the material, took a break, then reread the material again, over and over.

- Group two began with phase one revision. Next, they took a break and then generated some new examples to add to their learning (phase two) and finished by testing themselves on what they could recall (phase three).

- Group three also began with phase one revision. Then they took a break before going straight to phase three. They covered up everything they'd read and had to recall it without looking. Then they finished with phase two by generating some new examples.

Which group performed best in the subsequent exam? Here are the results:

Group	Technique	Outcome
One	Reread the material over and over.	39% gain on their original score
Two	Read the material, generate some new examples/ideas, then test themselves.	54% gain on their original score
Three	Read the material, test themselves, then generate some new examples/ideas.	62% gain on their original score

It's a really interesting finding. We can spend the same amount of time revising and get vastly different test scores due to the sequence of our revision. The conclusions here are clear – if you want to get the best outcomes:

1   Start with phase one revision (rereading, refamiliarising yourself).

2   Move onto phase three revision (cover your notes up, test how much you can recall).

3   Then finish with phase two revision (generate new examples, build new material).

THE BACKPACKER'S GUIDE TO REVISION, PART TWO

Welcome to the least fun sequel ever.

TWO WAYS OF LOOKING AT EFFORT

The tourist sees effort as a cost – something that must be spent in order to gain something else. It's transactional. Since no one wants to pay excessively, the tourist seeks to drive down costs. This leads to a bargain-hunting mindset. 'How can I pay the least amount possible for this?'

The backpacker sees effort as an investment – a downpayment that will pay dividends in the future. This leads to an engaged optimism. 'The more I put in now, the more my learning will pay me back later.'

There are a range of studies that examine these beliefs at play in students, summarised beautifully at the start of a paper by academics at a Dutch university. 'Students often continue to use ineffective learning strategies, such as rereading and highlighting, that on average lead to poorer learning outcomes,' they state, because 'such strategies ... are simple to use, low in effort and do not require much time investment.' (Hui et al., 2021, p. 1)

The tourist learns in a way that feels low-cost – the phase one and two work of rereading, checking textbooks, making a few notes and highlighting key terms. The backpacker, on the other hand, knows that revision should feel difficult, but that effort is an investment in future understanding. They challenge themselves, testing their understanding, pushing themselves to tackle difficult concepts and ensure that they truly understand them. If you want to *really* learn something, you need to seek out the difficulty of phase three revision.

Here, we propose three approaches to consider. We've sequenced them carefully – if you complete them in order, you'll do really well.

TASK

THE MOCK VIVA - EXPLAIN YOUR UNDERSTANDING OUT LOUD

A viva is a spoken exam: a way of testing student understanding and expertise, usually at postgraduate level in defence of a thesis. You aren't going to experience one any time soon, so don't worry. Imagine a kind of job interview. You will be asked to present your research to academics and talk, uninterrupted, about your subject. Then you will be asked questions which you must answer fully. A grade is awarded afterwards. Mocking one up is a superb way of learning something – a high-impact revision strategy which really helps embed your understanding of a topic and your ability to explain it fluently in your own words. Here's what to do:

▦ Prepare a ten-to-fifteen-minute talk on a topic. Only allow yourself to refer to a bullet-pointed list during the delivery; you shouldn't be reading a script. Transfer your main points onto a flash card. Then add three tricky questions that your imaginary viva panel – or study group members – are going to ask you.

▦ Then actually deliver your talk. Speak out loud in full sentences and academic language as if to a panel. Take the full time available. Finish by answering the three questions you've set yourself, aloud in full sentences, as if responding to your panel.

And you're done! You can complete an activity like this on your own, but it's even better when done with a group of friends, listening to and testing one another.

THE THREE Ts

In this activity, you're going to analyse and explore the very thing you're no doubt dreading: the test itself.

Track down as many example exam questions as you can find. Your lecturers will have shown you some. You might have seen presentations with example questions in them – trawl through your notes and print-outs until you find them. The VLE might have a store of past papers: download them all.

Now study them carefully, sifting through and reorganising them according to the three Ts.

The first T: topic

Go through the questions and get to grips with the kind of topics that you will be asked about. Have you got all the topics covered well enough? Are there niche topics that you're missing entirely? Are there topics that seem to come up over and over again? Obscure topics that are only asked about rarely?

Once you've finished your analysis, adjust your revision accordingly.

The second T: task

Any test or exam requires you to solve problems under timed conditions. So, what problems are you required to solve, exactly? Look for the command verbs in the example questions. Are you being asked to:

- **Define and describe things?** Look out for verbs like label, list, define, outline and summarise.

- **Explain things in detail?** Perhaps by showing how you work out a problem? Look out for verbs like determine, demonstrate, identify, calculate, show how and solve.

- **Analyse things, pulling them apart?** Look out for verbs like analyse, examine, explore, survey and investigate.

- **Justify opinions?** Look out for verbs like discuss, evaluate, assess, argue, justify and propose.

Once you've gone through your practice questions this way, you can double-check your confidence with each type of task and adjust your revision accordingly. Revising is about practising what to do with the information you've learnt.

The third T: toughness

Put all the questions you've gathered on a continuum, from what you personally find easiest to hardest, then take a step back and assess them. Ask yourself three questions:

- What topics and tasks are towards the easy end? You can reduce the amount of time you spend revising these.

- What topics and tasks sit in the middle? You'll need to spend a little more time on these, moving them closer to the easy end each time you work on them.

- What topics and tasks sit at the hard end? You'll need to take the time you'll save on the easy side and devote it to attacking this tougher stuff.

MICRO EXAMS

Some students think that they need to complete a full mock exam under timed conditions in order for it to 'count'. This isn't true. Rarely will you be able to find a quiet place and sit for two-and-a-half hours or more working your way through an entire past paper as part of your revision. Instead, try micro exams. Start small and build up:

- Take a single question. Calculate the amount of time you'd have to complete it. Set aside that time and attempt to answer the question under exam conditions.

- Gather a string of short-answer questions and do the same – see how you find jumping from question to question under exam conditions. Keep an eye on the time and get used to the pressure.

- Take a long-answer question and set aside twenty minutes just to see how it feels to get it planned and started under exam conditions. After twenty minutes, assess how you were doing. If it feels useful, go back into exam conditions and write one paragraph to double-check you're able to construct an answer under pressure.

The micro exam approach gets you used to the psychological and emotional experience of answering questions under pressure, without the long slog of a full paper. Make a habit of it and you'll be in a really strong position by the time the exam comes around.

PASSPORT STAMP – TAKE A BREAK AND EXPLORE THE COUNTRYSIDE

Intention – attend to your health and wellbeing by getting out into green spaces, leaving the noise of the city behind and exploring literal new pastures at a very low cost. Walk, bike, swim, or all three. Relax. Perfect for times of exam pressure!

Action – Look up the bus and train routes out to places of natural beauty within an hour or so of your university. The bus will probably be cheaper, but the train will be more likely to allow you to take a bike. If you are not sure where to go, search online for 'recommended walks', or similar, and check out reviews and photos. If still in doubt, look for National Parks, areas of outstanding natural beauty (AONBs), National Trust or Forestry Commission sites. If you live in central London, try the London Wetlands Centre or Kew Gardens (both are wonderful but expensive) or any of the eight Royal Parks, which are free.

Take a friend or two with you, wear appropriate footwear, dress for the weather, including sun protection, and bring plenty of food and drink. A paper map is a good backup in case of no phone signal, and it teaches you more about your surroundings. Ideally, in the UK, this would be from the Ordnance Survey Landranger or Explorer series. You can get these custom-made to centre on a specific place. An ideal going-to-uni present could be one of these, centred on your new home. Hint this to someone who loves you.

Reflection – do this reflection on top of a mountain, or deep in a woodland, or on a beach, or on the banks of a river. Watch the wildlife and the clouds go by and think about what this experience is giving you. Take your time. Many studies show how beneficial it is for us to spend regular time in green space – for example, White et al. (2019) found that spending at least 120 minutes a week in nature is associated with good health and wellbeing. The natural world is where we have evolved to be, so this is nourishing you on a very deep level. If you aren't feeling it, consider why. Are you cold, damp or hungry? Maybe you could have prepped better?

REROUTING – HOW TO SOLVE PROBLEMS AND PERSIST

Anyone familiar with travelling using online maps will know that when an obstacle appears on the road ahead, your satnav begins a process of rerouting.

Often, the traveller is shown three or four different *new* routes they could take to avoid the blockage. And these new routes come with new information – some cover more miles than others, some will save energy, some are quicker or slower.

Backpackers get used to rerouting.

When a problem occurs on their planned pathway, they switch paths. On more challenging journeys, they might have to do so three or four times: if the train line is shut, the last bus has gone or the road is flooded. At each obstacle, they generate a list of possible solutions, choose one and keep up their forward momentum.

But this kind of persistence takes practice.

Consider this example: a student calling in to a radio phone-in to explain why she dropped out of university. 'When I wanted to speak to someone about changing my modules,' she says, 'my personal tutor was nowhere to be seen.'[1]

A problem like this will inevitably happen to you too.

You'll encounter an obstacle on the road and need to reroute. The process, when mapped out, looks something like the table on page 122.

---

1   You and Yours, BBC Radio 4 (9 September 2014). Available at: https://www.bbc.co.uk/programmes/b04g8hrj.

Original route	Obstacle	Rerouting options	New route
I planned to …	But …	I considered …	And chose to …
Speak to my tutor to ask for some advice about how to improve my grade before handing in my work.	They were away at a conference for a couple of days and the deadline is tomorrow.	Asking my study group for help. Looking on the VLE for guidance on the assessment criteria. Finding some examples of previous work. Tracking down another tutor.	Find some examples of previous work, which I hadn't done before. It was a quick and easily available solution. I looked them over, got some ideas about what was missing in my work, and submitted on time.

The obstacles you encounter could be major or minor. Perhaps you can't access an essential piece of equipment that you need to complete a project. Maybe your laptop got broken, or you lost a crucial file, or got banned from the library when a study group session got out of hand.

The point is, you'll always have plenty of other options.

Tourists often give up as soon as an obstacle presents itself. The better ones might reroute once, then give up at the sight of a second hurdle. Backpackers, on the other hand, generate a whole host of possible solutions, then choose the best one in a decisive manner, even if it feels painful – whether it be requesting a deadline extension, loaning a university laptop, restarting the work from scratch or sending the librarian an apology letter.

You'll encounter plenty of study obstacles on this adventure. And your success will depend partly on your ability to reroute. It's a skill worth cultivating.

OFF THE BEATEN TRACK – MAKING CONNECTIONS IN YOUR LEARNING

One of the trickiest parts of travelling, and perhaps the most rewarding part of learning, is making new connections.

Let's say, for example, you are following three different modules at once, with lectures and seminars, workshops and tutorials, all taught by different staff and distributed across the week. Each module will have its own reading list, learning outcomes, assessments and so on. They can be taken as entirely separate entities, if you choose. There will be no overarching module called 'Psychology – How Everything Fits Together' or 'Archaeology – an Overview'. You can just get on with treating your modules as separate things.

On the other hand, you could choose to make connections between them and enjoy the benefits of expanding your understanding of each element of the course in relation to everything else. This is where the true creativity and joy of learning lies, and where you can make it your own.

Making connections is more than just having an overview. It is all about synthesis, which is a complex and high-level skill whereby knowledge and ideas are combined in different ways that are new to you, and may even be original, surprising, insightful or ground-breaking. It is intrinsically creative, and this applies whether you are studying a subject typically seen as creative – like art or fashion design – or something more factual, like a science.

If you are not sure what we are getting at here, we have a metaphor to hand. Picture your course as a hike through a forest. In this forest are several huge and ancient trees of various species, each of which represents a topic on your degree. You can always stick to the beaten track: a safe and well-worn path that will take you, one at a time, past each tree and allow you to experience them as individuals, in all their splendour. Stand and admire the unique bark and the shapes of the branches, the form of the leaves and colours of the fruit or flowers. At the end of that path, if you do it well, there will no doubt be a nice 2:1 waiting for you.

Or perhaps you step off the path and take a different view. Take a moment to look around you at how these individual specimens combine to form a forest: an ecosystem. Think about how each one relates to the next, aesthetically, spatially and underground through shared systems of roots, bacteria and fungi. Consider the effect the presence of one tree has on the life and being of another – maybe its neighbour, or maybe one on the far side of the forest.

What might stepping off the beaten track look like for you?

PART THREE
IN EMERGENCY BREAK SEAL

THE FIRST-TERM WOBBLE

. . . .

'He felt that his whole life was some kind of dream and he sometimes wondered whose it was and whether they were enjoying it.'
(Douglas Adams, *The Hitchhiker's Guide to the Galaxy*)

. . . .

Unfortunately, in the academic year ending 2024, around 41,000 undergraduate students dropped out of university (Jack, 2023). It's only one in
37, or roughly 3%, but this figure is on a steady upward trend.

If you're using the ideas in this guide, you should hopefully not be considering dropping out, but if you think that university might not be working
for you, just pause for a minute and take a breath.

Most new students have a first-term wobble. They've freewheeled
through the good times of the first few weeks, seen the sights and done
lots of new stuff. After a while, though, they could start to feel a few
doubts. They might be missing home and family. Or at least the dog. They

might start to feel worried about their own academic ability, or general direction in life, or money. It can feel lonely, like you are pedalling away on a long-distance path with nobody else around. Sometimes this leads to questioning whether you are on the right track at all.

If this might be you, this section is intended to help.

Think of this part of the book as the first aid kit that you carry with you throughout your adventure. Because, let's be honest, very few travellers get through a big expedition without incident. We focus here on study-related problems, but of course we know that these things are very often tangled up with all kinds of other difficulties that can be part of life. This book isn't big enough, and we don't have the expertise, to tackle all of those in depth, so don't forget that there are people all around you who want to help, as we showed you in **ACTIVITY 1.12** on page 69.

HOW DO I KNOW WHEN IT'S JUST A BUMP IN THE ROAD AND WHEN IT'S AN EMERGENCY?

Perspective will be important here. People have different reactions to risks and threats, and we would suggest that some difficulties are pretty normal occurrences for students and shouldn't leave you feeling overly concerned. As a very broad guide, for example, if:

- you miss a minor deadline by a couple of days
- you miss a few days of lectures due to illness, or
- you don't like the other people in your assessed work group

... then you've encountered a few bumps in the road. Put a sticking plaster over your minor cuts and bruises and carry on. These are the regular trials of any traveller – sometimes you're going to miss the bus, drop your guidebook in the river or get a common phrase badly wrong, like asking a Spanish speaker how many anuses they have (¿Cuantos anos tiene?) when you meant to ask how old they are (¿Cuantos años tiene?).

Don't punish yourself over these tiny hitches or blow them out of proportion. University is not about having a perfect academic record, so apologise to your teacher about the missed deadline, catch up on the work by watching lecture recordings, and grit your teeth and be nice to those troublesome colleagues in the assessed work group.

That said, you might encounter other difficulties which are less common and need swift attention.

The activities in this part of the book address problems that students do have now and again, which you'll need to attend to if they happen to you. We seriously suggest that you *don't* read this part in advance, in case you get the wrong impression. University is not a trip through uncharted wilderness, and you won't be beset by dragons, bears and sea monsters at every turn. Look at the contents page and see if any of the activities sound like they'd be helpful right now.

A NOTE ABOUT JOURNALING

One piece of advice when facing problems is that exploring your thoughts and feelings by writing them down in a personal journal can be very helpful. Many of the ideas in this book evolved from several years of journaling.

Writing about or drawing your feelings, ideas, plans and dilemmas can make them seem more self-contained and manageable. It can help you move towards objective detachment, which is helpful when reflecting and decision making. Or it can teach you more about yourself, which could support you in avoiding patterns of self-destructive behaviour.

An example of such behaviour is perfectionism. In our experience, this is a very common way in which students suffer: from the pain of 'failing' to meet the unrealistic standards that they have set for their own work. If you have been journaling, you can flick back through the last few weeks or months of your notes and seek patterns. Have you used language about yourself that seems negative? Are you critical of your own work and capabilities? Do you focus on relatively tiny aspects of your work or life?

We could give loads more examples, but the point here is that some of the problems we discuss in Part Three are the kinds of things that can be reduced or avoided by regular reflection, perhaps helped by a personal journal. And best of all, if you need to sit down and talk to someone about a problem, having journaled about it will help you to clarify what you have been experiencing and what you want to say.

ACTIVITY 3.1
ARE YOU FIT TO TRAVEL? WHEN NON-UNI PROBLEMS STOP YOU LEARNING

Many things can happen to us in life that make it hard to joyously explore new territory.

If your mind is full of problems, or you're physically struggling, or running out of money, these things can have a serious effect on your ability to learn. Relationship and family problems, or feelings of loneliness and anxiety, can happen to anyone and seldom respect your work schedule or deadlines. You could have followed all the methods in this book and worked your hardest but still find that you are not progressing as well as you know you can.

This section is just a gentle reminder to you, if you are in this kind of situation, that sometimes there are things in life that are even bigger than your education, important though it is. If you need time away to attend to those things, then take it. You might just need a few days of rest if you have been ill, or it could mean taking a longer break to spend time with someone who needs you. Perhaps it's more a question of taking some time to step away from your circumstances, examine your life from a distance and really think about why things are not working so well for you. If you are overcommitted or have financial problems, use this time to make a practical step-by-step plan. You might have some hard choices to make, but if you don't make them, you might not be fit to travel.

So do talk to that friend or counsellor. Stand back and see the problems as clearly as you are able.

This is a familiar idea, but a good one – consider what you would say if your good friend were in this position.

What help or advice would you give them?

DO YOU FEEL YOU BELONG?
WHEN IMPOSTOR SYNDROME STRIKES

Everyone experiences impostor syndrome.

That's an easy sentence to read and a difficult one to understand, so let's repeat it. *Everyone* experiences impostor syndrome. That means, at some point, your peers have, your friends have, your teachers have, the university counsellor has, the librarian has, and the canteen chef has – everyone has had a moment when they've felt like they don't belong:

- *I'm going to get found out.*
- *Everyone's better than me.*
- *I got lucky last time; this time will be different.*
- *The others are the genuine article and I'm just faking it.*

It's a near-universal feeling. Sometimes, it can turn into negative self-talk, so a simple expression of impostor syndrome, 'maybe I don't belong here', becomes 'I'm a total idiot.'

It's hard to backpack your way through a big adventure if you're telling yourself off all the time.

Writer and entrepreneur Seth Godin (2010) puts it well in a blog post titled 'The World's Worst Boss'. 'That would be *you*,' he writes, disarmingly. '*You* manage your career, your day, your responses […] your education, and the way you talk to yourself,' he writes, before adding: 'If you had a manager that talked to you the way you talked to you, you'd quit.'

He's right. So what can we do when we realise that we're beating ourselves up?

Spend some time reconnecting with your strengths and reliving previous successes. Politely tell the negative voice inside to pipe down. Maybe consider giving this voice a silly name that robs it of its power! Then mentally say to it, 'Thanks for your input. I've heard your opinion. Now I'm going to set you aside and think clearly and positively.'

Begin making a physical list of your strengths. What would your parents, siblings or extended family say were your positive qualities? Get everything out on paper. Keep thinking and digging, extend your list. You passed high-stakes exams when you were 16. Again when you were 18. You learnt challenging material, performed well under timed conditions, answered questions in class and successfully submitted your university application. You have determination, reliability, growing awareness and responsibility.

Once you've listed your strengths, try another list: the things you've learnt in the last month. What do you know now that you didn't thirty days ago? What technical terms, ideas, concepts or topics do you now know about? Look back over the list – at everything you've learnt. And you're only getting started! Imagine the length of those lists by the end of the semester.

Return to these activities if you ever feel like an impostor – they really help.

ACTIVITY 3.3
GOING SOLO – ARE YOU TRAVELLING ALONE?

There are times when we all want to be alone and, of course, times when we need to be alone. That said, a network of relationships and friendly faces is important on our travels. The word we want to emphasise here is *network*.

University isn't a sitcom: you don't need a gang of hilarious pals that you spend every waking hour with, and it's also not high school, so you needn't go searching for a best friend to attend every class with you. Universities are full of individuals: eccentric, interesting, engaging individuals. Some feel they have to join a style tribe or change who they are to fit in, but most students don't bother. They've waited long enough to be themselves and now they're going to embrace it.

So forget those ideas about meeting your perfect pals, soulmates or bosom buddies, and think instead about building a network – a range of acquaintances who you can grab a coffee and spend time with in different contexts and circumstances.

We suggest six places to start:

1   Use the opportunities you're given in class. You're bound to have a teacher who makes you discuss the work with your classmates at some point. Throw yourself into these experiences, even if it's not something you've enjoyed in the past.

2   Visit the cafes, canteens, study spaces and open-plan seating areas your campus provides. Get to know the ones next to your lecture halls and seminar rooms. If you're queuing for breakfast or picking up a drink, smile and say hi to the person next to you. This doesn't need to be an earth-shattering or life-changing experience. Take the pressure off yourself; you're not looking for your one true love, just being polite and approachable.

3   Attend a social event held by a club or society. If others seem to know more than you, it's the perfect chance to ask for help. ('So, what's all this about?' 'I'm new to this.' 'Do you mind just talking me

through what happens here?') If you have some interest and experience already, there will be like-minded people with whom you can share it.

4   Set aside the old rules about friendships – the high school rules that said you had to hang out with the kids in your year group. You don't. Your network might include students who are in year two or three of their courses, or even postgraduate teaching assistants. Strike up conversations about the work or ask for advice. ('What's the best cafe nearby?' 'How did you cope with finances in your first year?' 'What's it like living out of halls in the second year?' 'Any advice on how to approach [insert name of teacher]?')

5   Commit to listening. We're all human; we appreciate being heard. If you begin with, 'So, tell me about your home town. Where did you grow up?' and listen for as long as this person wants to talk, prompting them with questions, you can get to know a lot about someone relatively quickly. Really listen, and only jump in when it looks like they're running out of steam.

6   Help someone. Focusing on supporting someone else helps build a connection and takes you out of yourself and your own worries and concerns. Even if you can't answer a fellow student's query immediately, you might say, 'But I can help you find out if you want?' You could look for volunteering opportunities; your university might need student ambassadors for an event or someone to talk to a class of local schoolkids. You won't be the only one offering to help, and you'll meet new people as well as feeling positive about being useful.

ACTIVITY 3.4
ARE YOU LOST? IF YOU THINK YOU MIGHT BE ON THE WRONG COURSE

There could come a time at any point in the year when you feel you might be on the wrong course. When you chose this path, it seemed like the right way to go ... but now things have changed.

The possible causes of this feeling are many and varied, but it's worth pausing to reflect and consider how you have got to this point, and whether you'd be better off changing tack or sticking with the original plan.

It's time to interview yourself.

Go through our list, writing down the questions and answers that are as honest as they can possibly be. If this feels too daunting, you could ask somebody else to interview you, perhaps a parent or counsellor. Thinking over the following questions for a few days will give you time to consider whether this is just a passing feeling or one that requires action.

- What did I want from this course? Can I still get that from *this* course? Do I still want it?

- Is there time to switch courses at this uni in this academic year? How would I feel about doing this? Would I know what to switch to? Would the university allow me to switch courses?

- What is influencing how I feel about the course? Is it the content, the teaching, my fellow students, the difficulty level, my career direction or lack of it, my own skill set, or something else? Is it in my power to change how I feel about this, or could I change these circumstances for the better? If I could change it, would I want to stay?

- Is this a problem with the course, or is it the university, my own approach, or something else like housing, friendships or finance? Am I being bullied or discriminated against? If I leave, will the problem be solved or will I take it with me?

- Is university right for me? What are the alternatives, and would they be viable? Would they be fulfilling for me? Would they take me in the direction I want to go on my future path?

■ If I were to leave and apply for uni all over again, would this be affordable and would it be achievable for the course I want?

Look over your answers. Take time to think. Make sure you write down your answers so you know what you want to say when you have a conversation with someone about what to do next. And you *should* talk to someone about your feelings before you take any action. Parents, friends and professionals can listen and help you weigh up the pros and cons, and then it's your call.

Before you make any decision, it's worth reading about transfers on the UCAS website: https://www.ucas.com/undergraduate/student-life/ changing-or-leaving-your-course#transferring-to-a-different-course-at-the-same-university-or-college.

MISSING? IF YOU'RE GOING TO MISS, OR HAVE JUST MISSED, A BIG DEADLINE

If you can see a big deadline looming and feel there's no way you can make it, here is what *not* to do: plagiarise. Never, ever do this. If you think that AI is going to solve your problem, it isn't. Universities, unlike colleges, have sophisticated scanning software which tells them immediately how much of a submission has been stolen or AI generated. Soon enough they'll be sitting you down to explain why your grade is zero and you've been suspended from the course. Plus, you will learn nothing from cheating.

It's absolutely not an option.

Instead, you need to face the issue.

If you are too ill to work, or dealing with a tough life event, you might have to accept that you will have to do this work later in the year. Get a doctor's note and keep teaching staff informed of your situation. Check your department handbook or ask your tutor about applying for special consideration or exceptional circumstances. If that's not the case, you could consider all these suggestions, either in the following order or in the order of your choosing:

1   If you still have a few days before the deadline, speak to your teacher for advice. They want you to pass!

2   Seek help from peers, without going anywhere near plagiarism.

3   Prioritise tasks ruthlessly and cancel social events. Put other work on hold for a short spell.

4   Request an extension, using whatever official channels the course requires.

5   Pull an all-nighter or two – grim but could be worth it.

6   Complete the work to a lower standard than your usual, but good enough to pass.

If this works, and you meet that deadline, learn the lesson of how tough it was, but reward yourself with a treat. You pulled it back in the end!

If it doesn't, you simply can't complete the work in time and that ship has sailed:

1   Apologise to your teacher in writing or in person. They will appreciate this and perhaps offer support.

2   Face up to any extra fees you may need to pay for delayed submission of the work.

3   Reflect on what went wrong, accept responsibility (if it was your fault) and write down three resolutions to stop it happening again. To miss the boat once is perhaps unfortunate, do it twice and it starts to become a trend.

Lastly, if this problem was genuinely due to circumstances beyond your control, go easy on yourself.

ACTIVITY 3.6
LEFT BEHIND? HOW TO PICK UP THE PACE

This is a tough experience to have, especially if it persists over several months. Constantly feeling that you are behind your peers is exhausting and erodes your self-confidence. On the other hand, if you are always behind with work but feel totally unbothered, this is also a problem.

This situation won't resolve itself, so the time to act is now.

The reasons why you're lagging behind could be simple. You might already know that you spend too many evenings at your part-time job and lack energy as a result. In this kind of situation, hard decisions must be made, and quickly, before you get so far behind that you can't rescue the situation. What is your priority right now? If it is your academic work, then you have sole responsibility for refocusing your efforts. Can you cut your spending and your part-time work hours?

On the other hand, the reasons could be complex. They might include all kinds of intertwined issues from your personal, work and family life. If this is the case, we suggest that you reflect on the issues, write them down and divide them into things you can control and things you can't. This is an example list; yours might be quite different:

Issues within my control	Issues out of my control
Unstructured days	High workload
Distracting work environment	Illness
Disorganised programme of tasks	Caring responsibilities
Too much socialising	Family demands

First, consider the 'out of my control' column. Unfortunately, you will need to learn to accept the things you can't control, and not spend your time and mental energy on frustration, anger or feelings of injustice. Instead, you need to plan around these immovable factors.

Second, look at the issues within your control. These are the ones you can and should strategically tackle. Assess your circumstances, and have a look at the following list of possible ways forward to see if one might suit you:

- Change where you work, starting a new habit of studying in environments which promote concentration.
- Schedule additional study slots for yourself and treat them like non-negotiable timetabled sessions.
- Timetable yourself a catch-up week, where you schedule in work for every working hour of each day.
- Begin a 9–5 policy, where you stay on campus for the full working day and avoid the distractions present in your flat or room.
- If possible, temporarily reduce your hours of paid employment, explaining exactly why it's necessary to your boss, then using the gained time to study.
- Audit your screen time and commit to halving it by creating some parameters: 'I check social media twice a day on public transport only' or 'If I want to watch a programme, I'll sit down to watch it in the evening; I won't stream anything during my working hours.'
- Reduce procrastination by working in short bursts: a thirty-minute session can be powerful, so schedule short study sessions instead of telling yourself, 'There's no time to do anything!'
- Switch to a work-then-reward structure for your day, so that the things you love doing are saved until after hours and become rewards for engaging in study.
- Ground yourself. Being grounded – that thing where angry parents prevent a kid from going out because they behaved badly – is something you could usefully do to yourself. Impose new, stricter rules: you only go out socialising at weekends, for example. Use the gained time for study.
- Schedule early starts. Many students find the first few hours of the day are the best for focused, rewarding work. Check the opening hours for your building. Set your alarm for 6 am three days a week. Walk to campus and start work early. Some buildings have 24-hour access, but we would politely suggest that if you are regularly using this facility, you should take a serious look at your work–life balance.

If you think that your problem may be more to do with a loss of self-belief, have a look at the next activity, which may help.

ARE YOU STUCK? DO YOU FEEL FROZEN IN FEAR AND LIKE YOU CAN'T DO ANY WORK AT ALL?

As with the problem of feeling left behind, there could be complex reasons why you feel frozen, but one way to move forward could be reframing the feeling as a simple case of indecision.

Perhaps you feel that you have so many difficult tasks to do and so many deadlines to meet that you just don't know where to begin. Sometimes this can go on for too long and you become stuck in a state of denial or decision paralysis, unable to choose what to do next. But standing still is not an option, as it just makes everything seem worse. The backpacker makes choices, knowing that they must move on, trusting their own judgement.

So, here's your emergency guide to moving forward.

First things first: approach this task in a rested state, because decision making takes energy. List all the tasks on your mind, everything you have to do, all the actions you could take but are avoiding. Get everything out. Don't worry if this process takes a full hour or more – it's time well spent.

Now you have your list, it's time to place each individual task on our time–impact quadrant (see page 144). Replicate the box diagram on a blank piece of paper, nice and big.

First, assess the impact of the task. Imagine it was done and dusted. What impact would it have on your understanding? Positivity? Stress levels? Learning? Happiness? High-impact tasks are ones which would feel great to finish – they'd energise you and improve your understanding of the material. The higher the impact the task will have on your learning and confidence, the higher it goes on the impact axis.

Next, assess the time required to finish the task. Relatively quick tasks that could be finished in half an hour go towards the left. Bigger tasks that will take several hours go towards the right. If a task will take days or weeks, then you should break it down into smaller chunks and deal with those separately. Leaving it as one whole project is too daunting, and you just won't start it. Write each task in the appropriate square of the grid.

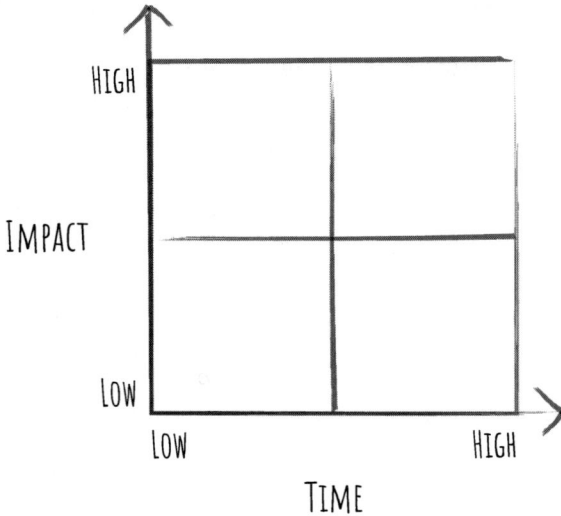

Now you've got tasks scattered around the four quadrants of the grid, you should have a greater sense of perspective about them all. It's time to make some assessments and take action.

DO A THING! A LIST OF PROMPTS

This is a range of options for you to choose from to get going again. Do them in any order – don't spend long deciding, just get started. And then, of course, do another thing. Repeat.

- Do a low-time, high-impact thing first. Do five more. Now you have built up some momentum.
- Do the quickest thing first.
- Do a thing for only ten minutes, then stop. Start again whenever you like.
- Do the thing that makes you feel the most positive. Give yourself a pat on the back.

- Do the scariest thing first. How great would it feel to have it done and behind you?

- Break a hard thing down into low-time sub-tasks and do one at a time.

- Do the fun thing first. It may be the easy option, but at least you've done a thing. Enjoy it!

- Get away from everything and everyone for a whole day (phone on aeroplane settings) and do three things.

- Break your habits – maybe work with a friend for a change, or tutor each other, or work very early in the day. Mix it up; you never know what might help.

ACTIVITY 3.8
WRONG WAY – WHEN YOUR FEEDBACK FEELS CRUSHING

We are reminded here of a trip to the USA where unfamiliar roadside signs on the freeway would simply state 'Wrong Way'. This actually means 'No Entry', but was amusing because of the sense of being told off by the big, red, block-caps road signs, with no further help offered, like what would be the better way?

When you first receive a disappointing mark and some critical feedback, it can feel like you're being told that you have done something very wrong indeed. Your tutor might have included some detailed, helpful feedback that could help put you back on track, but all you're seeing is the low mark and all you're hearing is WRONG WAY!

This is not unusual. From our own long experience of giving and receiving feedback, getting negative comments on your work can result in an uncomfortable trip through the following three emotional zones. It's best to acknowledge that this will happen to everyone. The aim of the following prompts is just to speed you on your way and remind you that these feelings are very typical.

ZONE 1 – HEART (HIGH EMOTION)

Journey time – anything from a few minutes or hours to a few days.

Journey stage – you have just received some very critical feedback, so you are responding entirely emotionally. You feel disheartened, angry, frustrated or humiliated. You might react as though you have been attacked by your teacher, rather than having had a piece of your work critiqued. You think:

- I hate them and they hate me!
- What do they know anyway?
- It's not fair; I worked so hard. This is an absolute disaster.
- I'm rubbish at this.
- I don't understand how/why this has happened!

In fact, of course, they do not hate you or indeed feel any emotion towards you. They are experts in their field so they know a lot more than you do. Nothing is ever fair (what gave you that idea?). You are here to learn, so if you are rubbish now then you can look forward to being way better by the end of the course. All of this will pass, and surprisingly quickly. If you are wondering what went wrong, that's good, because thinking about this will sweep you along into the next zone ...

ZONE 2 – HEAD (CONSIDERING WAYS FORWARD)

Journey time – two or three days.

Journey stage – you have got over the initial emotional reaction and cooled off. You know you need to form a rational and constructive response to the feedback. But you're still avoiding doing anything about it because part of you won't let go of the idea that you are not to blame for the negative outcome. You get together with your peers and question the task, dispute the marks and grumble about the phrasing of the written or verbal feedback you've received. This is resistance against taking action, and it feels uncomfortable. You think:

- They said give examples – and I did.
- They said I used poor technique – but I'm still learning this!

- They said I did insufficient research – but I spent hours on that!
- They said the essay was poorly referenced – does that really matter?
- They said the assignment was poorly structured – but it made total sense to me!

Now's the time to face the facts. Obviously, your examples were too few or not quite relevant, maybe both. Yes, you need improved technique, and that is what the feedback is intended to support. You either didn't spend enough time on research or it wasn't efficiently spent; perhaps you were using poor resources or researching superficially. Yes, accurate referencing matters very much. Look up the correct method on your uni's library website or VLE. If your work makes sense to you but not others, you need to take a step back and try to see it in a more detached way: leave it for a couple of weeks then look at it again with fresh eyes. You could ask a housemate or classmate to look at it for you or request some extra time with your teacher so they can talk you through any knotty problems.

Once you are doing this, you are already sailing over the border into Zone 3 ...

ZONE 3 – HANDS (GETTING DOWN TO WORK)

Journey time – anything from a week to a month or more, depending on the size of the task.

Journey stage – you are no longer quibbling about the assessment process and have decided to knuckle down and get on with it. Your actions will vary depending on whether the feedback was formative, and you have a final deadline looming, or whether it was summative, and you have just failed or barely scraped through a module. Whatever the situation, action is needed. For example:

- Make your own list of the weaknesses of the work – there might be more than the marker listed.
- Consult your study group or friends – ask to see their work if it was much better than yours.
- Either rework and resubmit (as needed) or make a reminder list of action points for next time.

- Be accepting of any element of sheer bad luck, such as illness – it happens.

- Move on to the next thing. When is your next opportunity to get some feedback? When you successfully cultivate this attitude, you have basically cracked the challenge of higher education!

You will probably find that your first-year grades do not count towards your final degree classification, but you might need to pass the year to proceed to year two. Your course handbook will likely be able to tell you.

ACTIVITY 3.9
STARTING AFRESH – LET'S TAKE THAT AGAIN

IF YOU FAIL A MODULE OR A YEAR

It might comfort you to know that 50% of your writing team found themselves in this situation after their first year at university. The course in question had a particular module that was tested at the end of year one – and entry into year two was dependent on passing. Things went very badly. Thankfully, there was a chance to retake, and it all worked out in the end.

So, what can we do when disaster strikes? The key, we've discovered, is to engage with it. This is the moment to wake up and face the issue.

OWN THE PROBLEM AND MAKE AN OBJECTIVE ASSESSMENT

Setbacks come with high emotion. When we fail, our emotions tend to come out in one of two ways: with a focus on external factors ('The university hasn't been good enough.') or internal factors ('I haven't been good enough.').

There is a problem with external justifications for failure. They result in long lists of reasons like these:

- 'No one ever explained how to write essays.'
- 'I was in halls with people who didn't do any work.'
- 'The lecturers didn't give me enough attention.'
- 'I couldn't find copies of the texts they recommended.'

Avoid this thinking. It prevents us from learning from failure, and instead gives us a story to tell about that failure. Worst of all, it implies that other students only passed because they were lucky enough to avoid the challenges that we faced.

The other way of thinking uses internal justifications for failure. This thinking is hard. It often begins negatively, with the student beating themselves up:

- 'University's not for me; I'm just not clever enough.'
- 'All I've managed to do is waste a whole lot of time and money.'
- 'I'm a complete disgrace – I've properly screwed up this time.'

But despite the pain, learning follows. Because whereas the external justification never changes – we double down on the story and tell it over and over again – internal justification is the start of a process of reflection. After the negative emotion comes honest self-appraisal. You might arrive at:

- 'It's true that my attendance could have been better.'
- 'If I'm honest, I should have asked for help – I've never actually met a teacher during office hours to ask for advice.'
- 'I wasn't always concentrating and taking notes in seminars.'
- 'I had too many hangovers.'
- 'I should have tried different learning spaces instead of getting distracted working in the student lounge.'

RUN A SIMPLE LAST TIME/THIS TIME ANALYSIS

Now you've taken ownership, assess what typified your study last time around, and plan immediate, reasonable and actionable changes. Here are a few examples:

Last time: I worked in the canteen, listening to music with my phone out, and stopped to chat with anyone who came past.

This time: I'll put my phone on aeroplane settings and study in the booths at the back of the library for an hour each day before lunch, then reward myself by socialising.

Last time: I skimmed the reading list but never really took it seriously.

This time: I'll assess the list carefully looking for the must-see texts (see **ACTIVITY 2.1** on page 75) and reserve one immediately in the library. At the start of each week I'll timetable a reading hour, where I'll read the key texts slowly and carefully, using Cornell Notes (see **ACTIVITY 2.2** on page 79) to summarise the main points.

Last time: I studied alone, often getting frustrated when topics were challenging and ended up trying to ignore them, hoping they wouldn't turn up in tests.

This time: I'll have a word with a friend and set up an informal study group once a week (see **ACTIVITY 1.10** on page 59), where we can review what's been covered, discuss it until it feels clearer, then test each other by explaining the content verbally.

VIVIDLY VISUALISE FUTURE SUCCESS

Now it's time to develop a mental picture of you engaging in these habits, and to imagine the positive benefits that will come from operating in this new way.

Write it down in the present tense like this: 'I'm studying hard; my grades are improving. I'm walking across campus, early for my next lecture, and I'm feeling much more positive and engaged. My stress levels are much lower. Later, I'm going to the gym and then out to see friends and I'm feeling carefree and on top of my work.'

You're picturing a process, not an outcome, creating a clear mental map to give you a vivid sense of what travelling well will look like for you. OK. You're ready to make some changes. You *can* overcome this setback, and you will.

ACTIVITY 3.10
TURNING BACK – WHEN YOU'RE CONSIDERING QUITTING

If you're reading this because you're thinking that you might abandon your journey and head home, here's the most important thing to know: you're not alone. In a recently conducted survey, the Higher Education Policy Institute interviewed 1,000 students and asked them if dropping out had ever crossed their mind. What percentage said that it had? 69% (Hanna, 2023)!

So, almost seven in ten students have had a moment when they consider that it might be quitting time. This thought is very common. Why? Well, it could be the result of a high level of challenge. It might be related to one of the problems addressed in this book – in which case, we hope there's something here to help you.

However, according to the survey, the majority of students cited finances as the main reason why they considered dropping out. They're either (a) running out of money, and they can't see how they can get any more, or (b) concerned about the debts they're accruing while studying.

If situation (a) describes you, there's help at hand. All universities have staff standing by to assist – so head into the students' union and explain what's happening. Do it today! Pretty soon, you'll be sitting down with a trained professional, and they'll be helping you fix things. Remember, over 50% of students have part-time jobs to help with their finances (Hanna, 2023), and the students' union often advertises job opportunities. Now might be the time to see what's out there.

Regarding situation (b), it's true that a combination of tuition fees and maintenance loans can make you feel like you're drowning in a sea of debt. But money expert Martin Lewis advises undergrads to think of that expenditure as a *tax* on their future earnings, not as a debt (Ungoed-Thomas, 2023).

In the UK, graduates earn more than non-graduates. The median salary for working-age graduates is £40,000, compared to non-graduates who earn an average of £29,500.[1]

Graduates don't start repaying their loans until they earn over a specific amount. The rules vary according to where in the UK you are from – for example, at the time of writing, the threshold is £25,000 a year in England[2] and £24,990 in Northern Ireland,[3] but £27,295 in Wales[4] and £31,395 in Scotland.[5] Once you earn more than this, you'll pay 9% of whatever you earn above that figure. That repayment percentage never changes; the amount you owe does not impact the repayment amount. It's always 9% above the earnings threshold. All this can change for new cohorts of students, so check for up-to-date information.[6]

Here are a couple of examples for clarity:

- If you are from England and have a job that earns you £26,000 a year, you pay 9% of the £1,000 you've earnt above the £25,000 threshold. That's £90 across the year, taken directly from your pay packet before you ever see it: £7.50 each month.

- If you are from England and earn £40,000 a year, you will pay 9% of the £15,000 you earn above £25,000. That's £1,350 across the year – £112 per month – taken from your pay packet before you ever see it.

You don't need to do any complicated paperwork. You don't need to inform anyone if you change jobs or if your earnings change. It's all dealt with for you. Finally, if you never pay it back in full, it's written off after a certain number of years: 40 years in England, 25 in Northern Ireland, 30 in both Scotland and Wales. When you reach this point, you stop payments regardless of how much you've paid off to date. The UK Government expects that around 65% of full-time undergraduates starting in 2023/24 will repay their loans in full (Bolton, 2024).

In summary, your loans are very much like a graduate tax, in that you're paying for your education after you have had it. The payments depend on how much you earn.

---

1   See https://explore-education-statistics.service.gov.uk/find-statistics/graduate-labour-markets.
2   See https://www.moneysavingexpert.com/students/student-loans-england-plan-5/.
3   See https://www.moneysavingexpert.com/students/student-loans-northern-ireland/.
4   See https://www.moneysavingexpert.com/students/student-loans-wales/.
5   See https://www.moneysavingexpert.com/students/student-loans-scotland/.
6   For more information about repayment plans, see https://www.moneysavingexpert.com/students/which-student-loan-plan-am-i-on-/.

If you leave half-way through your course, you will still have to repay the debt you've accrued up to that point.

OK, money section over.

The most important thing to remember is this: don't make your stay-or-go decision on the spur of the moment. It's far better to take a break first. Go home for a long weekend, reconnect with your family, check in with old friends and see how they're doing. Then...

Return to uni and set a deadline for your decision.

Commit to another month and take the pressure off regarding decision making. Throw yourself into everything during this month, attending lectures and classes, engaging with the work and looking for positives. Break out that trusty old notebook so you can start recording what's going well and what's concerning you. That way, you'll escape the heat and confusion of emotion and begin to see things more rationally.

Then, when your time is up, make your choice. For some students, dropping out is the right thing to do. There's no shame in this at all – all the social media platforms will include uploads from students explaining why they quit. Watch a few to see if they clarify your thinking.

And, if you choose to stay, reassure yourself: moments of doubt are normal in any journey.

ARRIVAL ... AND ONWARD TRAVEL

Thank you for reading this book!

We'd like to leave you with one last thought, looking ahead to when you graduate. Some of you will be academically outstanding and bound for a PhD and eventual professorship in your subject area. Others will be having a great time but just about passing their course. In the end, there is something that matters a lot more than grades.

Are you getting stuck into what you love doing?

What you love might not be what your course is about, and that's fine. A 2014 survey of 2,000 UK graduates undertaken by the New College of the Humanities, London, found that only half of them end up working in a field related to their degree (Garner, 2014). The rest? They've found new passions and interests to pursue, and their degree works as proof that they can organise and sequence work, hit deadlines, quickly gain expertise in new subjects and work independently.

Your degree will prove the same about you, so don't limit your plans or aspirations based on the course you've chosen. Here are a dozen famous examples ...

- TV archaeologist, anatomist and biological anthropologist Alice Roberts studied medicine.
- Astronaut Mae Jemison studied chemical engineering and African American studies, then became a medical doctor, before becoming the first African American woman in space.
- Documentary filmmaker and podcaster Louis Theroux studied history.
- Athlete Jessica Ennis-Hill studied psychology.
- Actor Liam Neeson began a degree in physics and computer science.
- Fashion designer Tom Ford studied architecture.
- Sir James Dyson studied furniture and interior design.
- TV presenter and comedian Romesh Ranganathan studied maths.
- Musician and singer Emeli Sandé studied medicine.
- Writer J. K. Rowling has a languages degree.

■ Albert Einstein trained as a teacher.

■ Actor, writer and comedian Miranda Hart studied politics.

Each of these people changed direction quite significantly from their starting point when they made their decisions about university. This is not a problem; in fact, it's a great strength to allow yourself to evolve and develop, following what makes you excited and exploring your own interests.

So, if you're studying art history but want to be an app designer, that ship has not sailed. Go ahead and design some apps. Do it while you're still at uni and can walk across campus and access all that expertise held by fellow students and staff. You might even make friendships or working relationships that will last for years to come.

If you're studying maths but you want to be an actor, have you joined the drama society and auditioned for student productions? University gives you that opportunity.

Do you want to be a journalist, but you are studying pharmacy? Your university will have a student paper. Write something!

Your authors have some experience of the post-graduation period. Neither of us made suitable choices straight away, and instead went for safe options, earning a regular wage being the only real criteria. We stacked shelves, wiped tables and just got by. We were a bit clueless and, looking back, could have planned better for the inevitable moment of leaving full-time education, so learn from our mistakes!

With this in mind, we'd like to leave you with three final challenges for onward travel.

1. ORGANISE AN INTERNSHIP OR SOME VOLUNTEERING

You can't be expected to plunge headfirst into a job pool without first testing the waters. Have a thorough look for established internship or volunteering programmes, at home or abroad. If they don't exist in the niche that you are looking for, why not set one up for yourself?

Even if you do something apparently random, you could still learn a lot from it. You might only intern or volunteer for a couple of weeks, or it could be for a whole year, but whatever you do, you'll be better-informed afterwards than you were before.

2. RESEARCH WHAT OTHER GRADUATES HAVE DONE

Every year, Prospects produces a detailed report called *What Do Graduates Do?*, which explores labour market trends and graduate employability. It takes the graduate cohort from three years back, tracks them for two years, then reports on the careers they've chosen. It's free to download, and the introduction provides you with a quick and helpful snapshot of what happened to those graduates once they finished their studies.

At the time of writing, the most recent report (Prospects, 2024) tells us that 80% of new graduates have gone straight into work, with the majority employed full time. We also see that 17% have continued to study in some way – almost half of them choosing to do a master's degree, a smaller cohort starting doctorates and some doing postgraduate certificates which give them access to particular professions – for example, teaching or law.

The bulk of the report is an in-depth look at the early career steps by graduates with specific degrees. It's worth a look if you're curious about what people do with that BA in philosophy!

3. TAKE A BREAK

You might have found your university experience quite demanding, especially towards the end. This means you might not be in a great position to make big life decisions. If you're feeling in need of a refresh, look for work experiences that seem like fun or are in an exciting new place. This next step doesn't need to be aspirational or a considered career move. You may need to give your brain a rest and afford yourself some space to reflect on your own talents and preferences before you decide what's next. This can take time, so don't rush. Stay curious and, most importantly, objective. Make a note of the activities, events, ideas or topics which excite or interest you, and treat them like clues to follow.

When you're well-rested, put your backpack back on and go and explore them.

And whatever you decide, we warmly wish you well. Get out there!

BIBLIOGRAPHY

Barrett, P., Davies, F., Zhang, Y. and Barrett, L. (2015). The Impact of Classroom Design on Pupils' Learning: Final Results of a Holistic, Multi-Level Analysis, *Building and Environment*, 89: 118–133. Available at: https://doi.org/10.1016/j.buildenv.2015.02.013.

Bolton, P. (2024). Research Briefing: Student Loan Statistics, House of Commons Library (5 December). Available at: https://commonslibrary.parliament.uk/research-briefings/sn01079/.

Bryan, C. J., Walton, G. M., Rogers, T. and Dweck, C. S. (2011). Motivating Voter Turnout by Invoking the Self, *Proceedings of the National Academy of Sciences* (PNAS), 108(31): 12653–12656. Available at: https://www.pnas.org/doi/full/10.1073/pnas.1103343108.

Conniff Allende, S. (2018). *Be More Pirate: Or How to Take on the World and Win* (London: Penguin).

Dai, H., Milkman, K. L. and Riis, J. (2015). Put Your Imperfections behind You: Temporal Landmarks Spur Goal Initiation When They Signal New Beginnings, *Psychological Science*, 26(12): 1927–1936. doi: 10.1177/0956797615605818

DeMarco, T. and Lister, T. (1999). *Peopleware: Productive Projects and Teams*, 2nd edn (New York: Dorset House Publishing Co.).

Evans, B. and Shively, C. (2019). Using the Cornell Note-Taking System Can Help Eighth Grade Students Alleviate the Impact of Interruptions While Reading at Home, *Journal of Inquiry and Action in Education*, 10(1). Available at: https://digitalcommons.buffalostate.edu/jiae/vol10/iss1/1.

Garner, R. (2014). Half of UK Graduates Do Not Work in Their Field of Study, Survey Reveals, *The Independent* (30 June). Available at: https://www.independent.co.uk/student/news/half-of-uk-graduates-do-not-work-in-their-field-of-study-survey-reveals-9574042.html.

Godin, S. (2010). The World's Worst Boss, *Seth's Blog* (4 December). Available at: https://seths.blog/2010/12/the-worlds-worst-boss/.

Hanna, L. (2023). Seven in Ten Students Consider Dropping out – How Can Universities Fix This Gloomy Statistic? *Higher Education Policy Institute* (2 March). Available at: https://www.hepi.ac.uk/2023/03/02/%EF%BF%BCseven-in-ten-students-consider-dropping-out-how-can-universities-fix-this-gloomy-statistic/.

Hui, L., de Bruin, A., Donkers, J. and Van Merriënboer, J. J. G. (2021). Stimulating the Intention to Change Learning Strategies: The Role of Narratives, *International Journal of Educational Research*, 107(2): 101753. doi: 10.1016/j.ijer.2021.101753

Humpherys, S. L. and Lazrig, I. (2020). Effects of Teaching and Practice of Time Management Skills on Academic Performance in Computer Information Systems Courses, *Information Systems Education Journal (ISEDJ)*, 19(2): 45–51. Available at: https://files.eric.ed.gov/fulltext/EJ1297703.pdf.

Jack, P. (2023). More Than 40,000 Students Drop Out of UK University Courses, *Times Higher Education* (28 September). Available at: https://www.timeshighereducation.com/news/more-40000-students-drop-out-uk-university-courses.

Katz-Vago, I. and Benita, M. (2023). Mastery-Approach and Performance-Approach Goals Predict Distinct Outcomes During Personal Academic Goal Pursuit, *British Journal of Educational Psychology*, 94(2): 309–327.

Kleon, A. (2013). Something Small, Every Day. *Medium* (30 December). Available at: https://medium.com/@austinkleon/something-small-every-day-c6ce326612c8.

Lawson, R. (2006). The Science of Cycology: Failures to Understand How Everyday Objects Work, *Memory and Cognition*, 34(8): 1667–1675. Available at: https://www.liverpool.ac.uk/~rlawson/PDF_Files/L-M&C-2006.pdf.

Levin, P. (2004). *Student-Friendly Guide: Successful Teamwork* (Maidenhead: Open University Press).

Maloney, D. (2024). The Importance of Reaching a Point in Your Day When You Feel Finished, *Dr David Maloney Psychotherapy* (28 July). Available at: https://www.youtube.com/watch?v=ZeFLBj8ZS-s.

Marmie, W. R. and Healy, A. F. (2004). Memory for Common Objects: Brief Intentional Study Is Sufficient to Overcome Poor Recall of US Coin Features, *Applied Cognitive Psychology*, 18(4): 445–453.

Newport, C. (2005). *How to Win at College: Simple Rules for Success from Star Students* (Crown Publishing).

Prospects (2024). *What Do Graduates Do? 2024/25* (Jisc/AGCAS). Available at: https://luminate.prospects.ac.uk/what-do-graduates-do.

Roelle, J., Froese, L., Krebs, R., Obergassel, N. and Waldeyer, J. (2022). Sequence Matters! Retrieval Practice Before Generative Learning Is More Effective Than the Reverse Order, *Learning and Instruction*, 80. Available at: https://doi.org/10.1016/j.learninstruc.2022.101634.

Scott Curry, O., Rowland, L. A., Van Lissa, C. J., Zlotowitz, S., McAlaney, J. and Whitehouse, H. (2018). Happy to Help? A Systematic Review and Meta-Analysis of the Effects of Performing Acts of Kindness on the Well-Being of the Actor, *Journal of Experimental Social Psychology*, 78: 320–329.

Sivers, D. (2020). *Hell Yeah or No: What's Worth Doing* (Sivers Limited).

Ungoed-Thomas, J. (2023). Martin Lewis: 'We Must Stop Calling It a Student Loan', *The Guardian* (13 May). Available at: https://www.theguardian.com/money/2023/may/13/martin-lewis-graduates-student-loans-finance-graduate-tax.

White, M. P., Alcock, I., Grellier, J., Wheeler, B. W., Hartig, T., Warber, S. L., Bone, A., Depledge, M. H. and Fleming, L. E. (2019). Spending at Least 120 minutes a Week in Nature Is Associated with Good Health and Wellbeing, *Scientific Reports*, 9: 7730. Available at: https://doi.org/10.1038/s41598-019-44097-3.

Wiseman, R. (2004). *The Luck Factor: The Scientific Study of the Lucky Mind* (London: Arrow Books).

Wong, B. and Chiu, Y. L. T. (2019). 'Swallow Your Pride and Fear': The Educational Strategies of High-Achieving Non-Traditional University Students, *British Journal of Sociology of Education*, 40(7): 868–882. Available at: https://doi.org/10.1080/01425692.2019.1604209.

Wong, S. S. H. and Lim, S. W. H. (2022). Deliberate Errors Promote Meaningful Learning, *Journal of Educational Psychology*, 114(8): 1817–1831. Available at: https://doi.org/10.1037/edu0000720.